WITNESS

WITNESS

by

JAMES CAMERON

LONDON
VICTOR GOLLANCZ LTD
1966

MADE AND PRINTED IN GREAT BRITAIN BY
THE GARDEN CITY PRESS LIMITED
LETCHWORTH, HERTFORDSHIRE

I have never dedicated a book to anyone before, but I would like to present this one to an old lady who lives in the village of Nanh Nganh, in the Thanh Hoa province of North Vietnam, which is unfortunately near to a strategically important bridge. The bridge, as far as I know, still stands, but the old lady had her left arm blown off by one of the bombs that went somewhat astray. She was more fortunate than her daughter, who was killed.

She said: "I suppose there is a reason for all this, but I do not understand what it is. I think I am too old now ever to find out."

The nations are as a drop of a bucket, and are accounted as the small dust of the balance.

ISAIAH xxxviii. 15

CONTENTS

FOREWORD

THIS BOOK IS the story of a journey made to North Vietnam in the winter of 1965, when the war that was distracting the south of that country was at its bloodiest and, it seemed, its most interminable.

Ordinarily it would have been a trip of no special acerbity nor moment—I had, after all, made it occasionally before—but the circumstances of the time gave it a curious importance, which had little to do with me.

For years North Vietnam had been closed territory, as far as observers from the West were concerned. Since the United States commitment in South Vietnam had grown and established itself into a condition of major war (and indeed for some years before that) virtually every major foreign correspondent of the non-Communist world had been hammering at the increasingly unresponsive door of the North, with a flat and total lack of success. Hanoi remained, to all intents and purposes, as inaccessible as Lhasa.

To this day I am uncertain as to how I pulled it off where other, and probably more deserving, people had failed. I was persistent to be sure, but so doubtless had hundreds of others been, arguing with the scattered consulates of the People's Democratic Republic in the very few Western countries that recognised the state or, even more awkwardly, in the Eastern republics. In a way it was like putting back the clock; I remembered only too well the almost identical experience with

China, fifteen years or so earlier, when Communist Peking was also a mystery, before China became part of the tourist map, to be trodden over annually by earnest seekers after the self evident. What were Chinese revelations in my day are now the commonplaces of statistical analysis. I waited three years for that visa.

I had to wait only about a third of that time for Hanoi, but it seemed long enough. At least a dozen times I despaired of the whole thing, and gave my mind to other enterprises offering a more reasonable chance of making a living, which has always been a serious preoccupation of mine. Then—exactly as with the first Chinese visa, so long before—when the permission came, it arrived abruptly, out of the blue, and with the insistence that it be taken up immediately. There is something almost admirable in the bland attitude of assurance that enables these administrations to say, in effect: well, since you seem so keen to come, then come; but you must arrive in three days' time or the deal is off.

There was of course the question of raising the money, getting the passages, organising the equipment; but this was my concern, not Hanoi's.

Why I was selected out of the clamouring multitude of serious newspapermen remains, as I say, an enigma to me; it could have been the fact that throughout the operation I had insisted on going, if I went, on my own terms. It seemed to me to be necessary that for such a tricky mission—from which, after all, many responsible and accredited diplomatists had been barred—I should go uncommitted and unsponsored, as nobody's guest and nobody's delegate; I should go without obligations or responsibilities. Nobody sent me; I was answerable, whatever happened, to nobody but myself. It was a situation practically unique in these days of expensive foreign correspondence, the elaboration of film units, and the compulsions of a head office. I had none of these; the risks scared me to death, but it came off.

In the end, then, I got in. I saw Hanoi again for the first time since I was there, in the twilight of French Indo-China, writing about its dissolution in the *News Chronicle*—itself, alas, destined not to outlast the French empire for long.

I am a Westerner; I have spent much of my life in odd and improbable places, and I have become deeply attached to Asia over the years; yet I remain a European even by inclination. I can hardly pretend that this narrative is the "truth" about North Vietnam; an experience of this kind is unlikely to produce a heavy harvest of the eternal verities. Still, I travelled about the country; I did not see everything I might have wished to see, but I saw a great deal more than has been seen for a long time.

It is possibly apparent that I am not a Tory; I hope it is equally obvious that I am not a Communist; I am in a condition of galloping disenchantment with the Labour Party; my personal political loyalties have yet to find an established party home. I should nevertheless make it clear that I think the existing American-Vietnam war is both imbecile and brutal, and as I hope to make clear the chief charge against it is that it is corrupting both sides—not equally, but in some cruel and unnecessary measure. I hate all wars (and for twenty-odd years I seem to have been mixed up with far too many) but especially do I hate this one.

I am not writing a pamphlet; all I am trying to do here is explain what I saw, and recount what I heard.

ON THE WAY

AT FIVE IN the morning Peking has a disembodied air; its strange pearly quality achieves no sort of shape in the half-light; its outlines are blurred and misty; it is rather like existing within a seventeenth-century Chinese water-colour. It is lovely, but eerie.

It had been years since I had last been in Peking, which is a city with uncommon charm for me. I was so entranced at being back again, if only momentarily, that I could hardly bring myself to go to bed. In any case the plane for Vietnam was to leave at dawn. I fussed and wandered about imprudently for hours. I thus missed, though I did not know it, the last chance of any serious night's sleep I was to have for weeks.

You have to be up extremely early in the morning to beat the first Chinese; in fact I doubt whether it is possible. Long before dawn there is always someone about sweeping the streets or pushing a barrow or shuffling stuff behind the shutters of a shop. Peking is a curiously un-animated city, but it never really goes to sleep. At five that morning the blue lines of workers were already lining up for the early buses. A few zealots writhed about under the trees doing their obligatory morning PT. The public loudspeakers that are the one indefensible curse of that agreeable city were already in business, braying out Slavonic martial music and the erratic wail of Peking opera. It was all very like it had been in the old days.

By the time I got to the airport the day was fully under way. Peking airport is a place you seem to be at only in the middle of the night or at the crack of dawn; it has the vaguely neurotic feeling of those sections of a Communist city that are used almost wholly by foreigners. All airports have a queer dissociation from the ordinary life of the cities they serve; Peking's could be in another world.

By some sort of Oriental paradox it is a big job getting one's *dokumenti* attended to in China. It is necessary to stand around in great echoing halls under immense busts of Chairman Mao, apparently cast from one universal mould in some pallid material resembling lard, until someone comes and asks you, almost diffidently, for your passport. There would doubtless be the most unholy trouble if you contrived to miss the formalities (as most fearfully did I find out on the homeward trip) but the administrative procedure seems oddly casual. At that time of day nobody speaks English, and there is much cordial misunderstanding. The only thing to do is to produce every kind of form and document in one's possession and proffer the lot; the official accepts them with a puzzled air and goes dreamily away into invisibility, leaving one rooted to the spot, not daring to move in case he never finds one again.

Eventually one is always rescued by a very young woman with her pigtail in a bow, who copes with the situation. Contemporary China gives the impression of being managed entirely by very competent schoolgirls.

My flight was going to Wu-han and Nan-ning and thence to Hanoi, which caused a certain interest; it is not every day that British passports go to North Vietnam. My immigration official was suitably inscrutable; he took the thing as no great drama (which it certainly was to me), rather did he appear to regard the trip as a quaint eccentricity.

"Hanoi, ha-ha," he said. "You go wrong way."

I had a moment of great alarm, thinking I might be mistakenly embarking on a flight to Vladivostok, until I remembered the Chinese trouble with the letter "l".

"Yes, a long way," I replied.

"Don't mention," said the officer enigmatically, and gave me a card that said "Valid for One Muslim Meal."

* * *

They soon forgot about me, however; they became too busy with the Russians.

Somehow the departure lounge had become full of Russian experts (every Russian outside Russia is by definition an "expert") who were milling about in a kind of disciplined confusion, shouting loud instructions at each other and pacing about in all directions without at any time ceasing to be a cohesive group. This is a procedure which in my experience is peculiar to Soviet travelling parties: that of separate people busying themselves in intensely individual activities while never for an instant losing touch with the *ensemble*.

They were a group of Soviet technicians bound for North Vietnam—almost certainly mechanics for the anti-aircraft missile-sites with (as it turned out later) a few advisers in civil engineering. It was one of the hazards of their exacting trade that to reach their destination from Moscow they were obliged to travel through Peking. There was no welcome for them there, and they knew it.

As we entered the aircraft we were presented with handfuls of small, densely printed, and very hostile booklets. There are many delights to be found in the People's Republic of China, as well I have found, but the distribution of public reading-matter is not one of them. It has been a frequent penance for me to be left with nothing to read but the numbingly boring propaganda pamphlets that abound, and which are even less rewarding when all that are left on the stands are the versions in Swahili or Albanian.

I found myself left in the plane with only a booklet crisply called: "We Shall Fight to the End against Khrushchovism, Soviet Revisionism, and Moscow's Betrayal of the World-Wide Struggle against Imperialism." The alternatives were "Down for Ever with Moscow's Philosophy of Splittism," or "The Soviet-US Conspiracy: a Study in Treachery." They seemed flashy things to be reading in a planeful of Russians, even though it was a Chinese plane; it is curious what a sense of ideological neutralism comes over one, surrounded by Soviet citizens ten thousand feet above Shansi Province. The Chinese had considerately provided every Russian with a selection of the most vigorously anti-Soviet literature in stock.

My seat companion was very civil; he was thumbing without excitement, since he could not read it, through "Le Trahison des Héritiers de Khrushchov." He was an extremely huge man; I wondered what service he was going to render to the people of North Vietnam. Then the comrade stewardess brought the tea round; the glasses were so horribly hot that I nearly screamed, and dropped mine on the gangway. My companion reached out a hand that must have been made of the material of a hoof, enveloped the almost incandescent glass, and sent the whole boiling lot down in one.

There was one great diversion. Soon after take-off a fly appeared, wandering distractedly around the cabin. This, in China, is always a great event, as I remember from early days in Peking; I was gratified to see that things had little changed. The great phenomenon then had been the famous "fly campaign," part of the great drive for the most un-Chinese cleanliness and hygiene, when no fly's life had been worth a moment's purchase. For years thereafter any stray fly that had somehow escaped the original purge was harried remorselessly, and such was the case with this one, entrapped in the Hanoi plane. The anti-fly attitude has clearly become a conditioned response, and the comrade stewardess reacted dead on cue. Magically there appeared in her hand a People's fly-swatter, and the hunt was up. As the fly felt obliged to settle on the back of a seat it was taken out, as the Americans say, with a deft and practised forehand flick, and its remains wrapped in a piece of paper and taken away to wherever Chinese flies go after death.

This caused a great flurry among the Russians, who had clearly heard all the funny Pekinese fly-stories; they applauded loudly, with what I could not help feeling was a strong undertone of satire. Then they affected to find flies everywhere, and for a while there was much happy horseplay, with the Soviet passengers scrambling about and swatting each other on the head with rolled-up sick-bags. This was their revenge for the pamphlets. The comrade stewardess looked on impassively, but I saw she kept her own professional swatter at the ready from then on.

"The intractable divergences between the Marxist-Leninists and the schismatic faction of the CPSU," I read in the Peking pamphlet, "rest on the question: do we ally with the labouring people of the world against the American Imperialists and their lackeys, or do we ally with the American Imperialists and their lackeys against the labouring people of the world? Among the many acts of betrayal committed by the Khrushchovian revisionists the most flagrant was the conclusion with the US and the UK of the shameful Treaty on the partial cessation of nuclear tests, the great act of treason against the peace-loving peoples of the world...."

I read it once, and twice, and indeed again; it said the same thing every time.

We were over the Yiangtse Kiang; we were over Hunan Province into Kwangsi, over the lush and abundant South China; invisibly down there were the patchwork fields of rice and sugar, the buffalo drowsing in their pools and the farmers turning the irrigation treadmills. For a moment I wished I were going back there, and not going into the unknown bafflements of Vietnam.

At Nan-ning is the frontier. I still had in my possession twenty-four pieces of People's money—twenty-four yuan, Y24: about £2 10s. It is illegal to export the smallest amount of Chinese currency; I deposited the money in the Nan-ning airport branch of the Bank of China, against a receipt that took ten minutes to prepare.

"I am now," I said, "in a sense, a capitalist of China."

The man smiled wanly, and returned to his abacus. In China there are things too trivial even for jokes.

A couple of hours later I was in Hanoi.

In such a mood shall men land on the moon.

THROUGH THE LOOKING-GLASS

FIRST IMPRESSIONS ARE everything; only too quickly do the edges become blunted, the vernal surprises fade into the commonplace; in a week you have forgotten the urgency of that first day's revelation, too soon is life overrun by the banal frustrations of ordinary survival. It is very important to write as you go along.

In jeeps and by the sides of roads; in guest-house bedrooms and the bleak departure lounges of obscure airports; in notebooks until they are full, and then on the backs of unanswered letters; too often when minor emergencies distract the mind, or fatigue has numbed the words. It is the negation of creation; if art is emotion recollected in tranquillity, journalism is the fugitive notion recorded in uneasiness and discomfort. It is in general an unfulfilling trade, yet it is possible that it may have its occasional usefulness.

From North Vietnam I wrote:

"When the sirens go these days there is a difference: the shelters are made of earth and seem built for children, the loudspeakers chatter their warnings and exhortations in Vietnamese, so that I am unable to distinguish whether I am being urged to run like hell or merely improve my production. Moreover the men in the planes overhead are surely called Bill, or Joe, and are already thinking about getting back for lunch aboard their carrier in the Seventh Fleet. Maybe they will and maybe they won't. I am ill-accustomed to being bombed by Americans.

"Not so the people here in North Vietnam; indeed this is the one thing that obsesses them. Every aspect of life is dominated by this mood of embattlement and siege. It is tangible everywhere in the eerie emptiness of the daylight countryside, the emphasis on darkness, the air-raid shelters and foxholes, the rifles stacked at the corners of paddy-fields and the edges of desks, the great painted posters everywhere proclaiming bitterness and defiance.

" 'We are, as you know, in a state of war'—it explains everything, excuses everything: the hardships, the rationing, the endless repetitive hours of civil-defence rehearsal and AA drill, the anger that keeps breaking through the gentle courtesies. Sometimes, as with ourselves in wartime, it excuses too much—the regimentation, the sudden bursts of suspicion, the barrenness of everything, the exaggeration of both suffering and success. But no wonder, you say, as you look at this unhappy and furious country, no wonder; no people in the world have been so continuously at war as these small people of Vietnam."

There is an amount of certain hindsight in that; in those early days in Hanoi I had heard no sirens sound, as it were in anger, though there were plenty to come. But there can be no dispute over the last phrase, for indeed it is true that the travails of war have troubled these people for generations. Vietnam seems to be one of those vulnerable yet prickly countries, like Cyprus, that have been forever contesting the intention of others to absorb or overcome them. Two millennia ago they were fighting against the Empire of Siam, which in those days was considerable, stretching from the

Thai country into South China. They battled for centuries against the Chinese, as an independent nation until their absorption into the Chinese Empire at the start of the fifteenth century. The components of what came to be known as Indo-China—Laos, Tonkin, Annam, Cambodia—were at odds with each other for a thousand years. Someone or other was, at almost any recorded period, attempting to swallow Vietnam; it is a most curious and interesting historical fact that no one ever contrived permanently to succeed. Much of this fact may be accounted for by the inevitable ebb and flow of power politics, but even more must be explained by the singular resilience and continuity of the Vietnamese, who are, despite the graceful and beguilingly diffident tactfulness of their demeanour, among the toughest and most unanswerable people on earth. It is a fact that, surrounded by all this charm, all this almost irresistible accommodation of character, one can too easily overlook the basically iron factor in their political nature. A Vietnamese told me the other day: "You overrate this quality of sweetness in the Indo-Chinese nature; we are brutal at heart. At least to each other. What is going on in the south of the country couldn't otherwise be conceivable."

One felt extremely alone in Hanoi. Among its 600,000 inhabitants there seemed to be nobody like oneself—nor was there, nor had there been for years. It had been far from easy to get there; the thing was virtually unprecedented, and felt it. This was not a place where non-Communist Westerners were welcomed, since recently the only ones who had come had arrived in B-50s and F-105s and blown things up, like bridges and people, which was not agreeable when you saw it, nor indeed very persuasive. My European face was accepted so long as I was taken to be a Russian technician or a Czech diplomat; when they learned who I was the reaction was astonishment, curiosity, and doubt.

But one was through the looking-glass at last, in the capital of North Vietnam, in Hanoi, which the Americans will say is full of demons and the Communists will say is full of heroes. It seemed to me, on the contrary, to be very full of people, largely indistinguishable from those of Saigon except in the bleak austerity of their condition.

The important thing was that one was now *through* the looking-glass, and everything outside—home and London and New York; everything—was now a sort of mirror-image, where black was white and white was black, good was bad and bad was good, defence was aggression, military efficiency was wanton cruelty, right was wrong. It was not the first time this had happened to me, but more strikingly now than ever before. Once you turn all the political value-judgments into terms of people, they become both simpler and more difficult.

The Hanoi that was once the pretty, indolent, rather charming French colonial town of *mes petites Tonkinoises*, and the Hanoi that is the capital of the Democratic Republic of Vietnam are twelve years apart in time and an infinity of mood. To see it again after such an age was like revisiting some bibulous old coquette of a Tante Marie and finding her reformed and censorious, barren of make-up and busy in the WVS. One was obliged to admire, but one was not beguiled.

I remember the place from my sojourns there in the days of the last cynical rearguard actions of General Navarre's Army—its pleasant tree-lined avenues, its parks set around the Three Lakes, its air of congenial and slightly shabby decadence. In those days we were waiting for the end of the last French empire, already on its deathbed at a place called Dien Bien Phu. It was not a name many of us knew at the time.

Now it is the name of one of the biggest thoroughfares in Hanoi. What used to be the avenue de Lattre de Tassigny has been rechristened Dien Bien Phu Street. I find a certain significance in that. They did not call it Lenin Street, or Karl Marx Street, or even Ho Chi Minh Street; they called it Dien Bien Phu Street, because that part of the revolution was wholly and undilutedly Vietnamese.

How it had changed. No more brilliant girls floating like butterflies in their gossamer *ao dai* gowns, the flowing silk pyjama and the deep-slit robe; the uniform of the workers was everywhere: black trousers, tightly buttoned white jacket.

Even in its colonial heyday Hanoi was never a place of very rich diversion, but it had some agreeable places. I looked quite eagerly for things I had remembered, but could no longer find—where was the Restaurant Manoire, and the little Bar Paradis, where the taxi-dancers sat embroidering, demure as schoolgirls: what had they become? They had become nothing, it seemed. They had not just been transformed, or closed; they had ceased ever to have existed, and nobody remembered ever having heard of them. I had expected them to say that such enterprises were unhelpful to a democratic society, and that they had been turned into crèches, or Street Committee Halls—but no; they were part of the colonial past, they had been written out of memory.

What of the dreadful Maison de la Presse, where I

had been so distressfully lodged as a temporary appendage of the French Army, yearning for the forbidden luxuries of the Hôtel Métropole? It, too, had become a non-thing; it had never been. Useless for me to protest: "But I was *there*; I *remember* everything about it, except where it was." They would look at me with considerate incomprehension. "You really must be mistaken."

Instead, I was now sent to inhabit the Métropole. It had become the Thong Nhat, the Unity Hotel, and whatever were its former glories in the days of General Navarre, they had departed. They could not, in any case, have been exceptional. It had now the unmistakable air that characterises hotels in People's Democracies the world over: a greyish patina of the slightly forlorn and inhospitable, the rejection of all the accepted innkeepers' values in favour of the stark and utilitarian. It is not easy to describe this rather bleak condition, which probably has less to do with socialism than with carelessness and inattention; it comes when an institution intended for the use of the convivial and discriminating is adapted for the use of the dedicated and austere; it has quite a forceful symbolism. It reveals itself in a kind of efficient run-downness, what can only be called a sort of calculated shabbiness. It is not warming, but it works. It was, after all, exclusively the "foreigners' hotel." One felt its charmlessness would not greatly appeal to the Vietnamese.

The staff were courteous and efficient. The rooms were ready; would monsieur ascend at his convenience, and to the account of which ministry should the bill be charged?

At this point arose the situation that I have encountered all over the Popular Democratic world: I had to dispel the illusion that I had arrived in the country as an accepted guest, explain that on this occasion there was no department or section to pick up my checks, and that on the contrary I was paying for myself. I have observed that in such establishments, where almost every guest is precisely what the word means, as a delegate of something or a member of something else, the actual machinery for relieving visitors of real money tends to creak. However, it was a point of some importance that I should not be a guest on this occasion; I remembered only too well how William Warbey, MP, had been sold down the river on that score after his visit to Hanoi, all his arguments and protests vitiated by his opponents' insistence that, as an invited guest, he could hardly be considered an objective witness. I was going to pay if it killed me.

Downstairs, at the sombre bar—the only one, it seemed, in all Hanoi—brooded a handful of expatriates: Rumanian attachés, the Soviet cultural officer, a few East Germans, the man from Tass. They received me initially with a certain dubiety, tempered by great curiosity, and the mild excitement of having a stranger who, Western imperialist running-dog in disguise as he might well be, was at least someone different to talk to.

I would not say that during my stay our acquaintanceship ripened perceptibly, but I made one congenial friend: a splendid unsinkably sanguine Bulgarian with brilliant eyes in an actor's face; he introduced himself to me with great drama. "I have just heard the radio; the news from Europe is disastrous, catastrophic!" He eagerly awaited my reaction, which was stunned; I had heard nothing for days, anything could have happened. Aghast, I begged to be informed.

"It is the European Cup, what else. Bulgaria has been beaten five-nothing—*imaginez-vous, par les Belges!*"

He smote his brow, observing me narrowly. I took the cue and wrung my hands in outrage. Thereafter, whenever we met, I was obliged to manifest an interest and simulate a knowledge of football, a subject of which I am almost totally ignorant—or should I say that I was; I am less so now.

The bar was tended by a Vietnamese lady of what in the early days seemed to be most agreeable charm, and later of almost unendurable attraction. She was known to the melancholy diplomats as "Madame Beautiful"; she accepted the epithet with a weary and practised resignation. Her duties were uncomplicated, since there was virtually nothing to drink except the Vietnamese local spirit called *Lua Moi*, a variety of Asian vodka that is probably the only thing that is slightly more corrosive than the Chinese *mao t'ai*, and certainly the only alcoholic drink I have found, in long and diligent search throughout the world, that I found difficult to take. Sometimes the Vietnamese would pour it into a saucer and set a match to it, whereupon it burned with a fierce and penetrating flame, and on this they would toast a local variety of dried squid, of which many connoisseurs thought highly. Such were the gastronomic highlights of the Unity Hotel.

My room was vast, and of a scrupulous cleanliness that I am perfectly certain did not exist in the days of the Occupation Army. The bath had five taps, all unmarked except one, which said "Froid." This was the one which emitted boiling water for one hour a day. It was not much of a hotel, but it was, of necessity, home. Later, in the bush, I was to think of it almost with yearning.

Outside, the war hung overhead like a brutal cloud. The schools had been evacuated from the towns; I was to see more of this. While I was in Hanoi there took place a strange and fanciful ceremony: the formal opening of the new Polytechnic University, which had been donated and constructed as a gift entirely by the Soviet Union, and a very impressive establishment it was, to be sure, with corridors of laboratories equipped with all manner of elaborate machinery. The ceremony was graced by the presence of the Vietnam Minister for Universities and Higher Education, and by his counterpart from Moscow; there were hours of vigorous oratory and many distinguished guests in the auditorium. And the moment the ceremony was over, the university closed down. There was something both paradoxical and pathetic about this: the gesture of opening the city's first major seat of learning in the middle of a war, with the accepted knowledge that, because of the evacuation, it could admit no students at all until the war was over.

One returned into town, a little cast down.

At once one was beset by bicycles. Never did I see such a bicycling town as Hanoi; not even Copenhagen, not even Amsterdam; the whole city rides on two wheels. The streets are peopled by thousands of bikes: one-man bikes, two-man bikes, even on occasion three-man bikes, a meandering river. It made crossing the street on foot a singular hazard; infinitely sooner would I cross Oxford Street or Madison Avenue in the rush-hour; at least automobiles do not swoop and whirl capriciously; hateful though cars are, they have a predictable pattern. In Hanoi the stream of traffic is almost eerie by being at the same time so dense and so silent.

The thousands of machines come from China, from Czechoslovakia, not a few from North Vietnam itself. There were frequent collisions. After each one the collapsed parties did not curse or even remonstrate, but picked themselves up in a murmur of mutual apology.

The markets still flourished, in a curiously new and aseptic way, since the Market Co-operatives and the Women's Union got to work on them four years ago insisting on the novel virtue of hygiene, and good order, and price control.

Since so many families had been divided and disrupted by evacuation there had been a useful innovation in the "street kitchens"—you deposited your stewpot in the morning and collected it later, ready cooked. The Vietnam people are most mutually dependent; it shows itself in their tendency to walk around hand in hand; it is a very decrepit bicycle indeed that does not carry two or even three people, and no child is too small to have an even smaller on its back or in its arms.

North Vietnam was littered with broken bridges and pulverised roads, but the bridge over the vast Song Hong was intact, spanning the mile-wide Red River that is, indeed, red: a great warm stream of tomato soup. The waters were receding in the dry season; as the banks of silt appeared the peasants descended on them, and cultivated them; they could get a crop off them before the rains returned and drowned the plots.

In the pretty parks by the lakeside were glass showcases of pictures from what are called the "other comrade countries." Their names read oddly, transliterated into the tonal monosyllables of Vietnamese: Hun-ga-ri, Ro-ma-ni, Bun-ga-ri, Cu-ba, Ce-sko-wak.

But the centrepiece was the board—in a fanciful way it was like a cricket score-board—that announced the daily figure of US planes shot down. That day they claimed no fewer than ten—in one day, could it be possible? The design on the board was the ubiquitous one of the peasant girl laying down her reaping-hook and pointing her rifle dauntlessly at the sky. One knew it wasn't all done by rifles, but the gesture is important.

I found the figure hard to swallow. Ten in a day! "J'espère qu'ils sont des prisonniers." "Pourquoi?" "Parce que—je suppose qu'on a eu assez de la mort." We stared at the score-board, turning war into mathematics, as we did twenty-five years ago in England in the days when it was our turn. It is part of this oblique fantasy that the Vietnamese word for aircraft, when it is not officially "rabid-imperialist-aggressor," is almost coquettish: *may bay*.

Civil defence rehearsals happen all the time. I saw them in the fields of the farm co-operatives, where the alarm was given dramatically on a drum; in the car-repair factory, where it was sounded on a very old empty French bomb.

The constant emphasis on rifle-drill had a serious purpose obviously not wholly connected with shooting down US planes. The idea that an F-4B Phantom bomber flying at 1,500 m.p.h. can be vulnerable to a pretty little peasant girl with a musket is so implausible that serious Vietnamese dislike debating the subject. Doubtless in the early days after "escalation" some US pilots took the risks too lightly and dawdled somewhat over these harmless paddy-fields, and certainly were destroyed with rifle fire. The necessarily steep angle of dive-bombing also makes them a momentarily good target for a very intrepid machine-gunner.

But clearly a great number of the stricken planes were destroyed by sophisticated AA equipment, and the Russian-installed SAM missiles which dot the countryside, serviced by the Soviet technicians one occasionally met on their rare binges in the city. Twice I passed these things, shrouded in the darkness. No one discussed them.

The endless rifle-talk was certainly psychological. It consoled the peasant into a sense of positive activity, of sharing; it was an invaluable means of channelling off his frustration. It was a powerful part of civilian morale. Every Village Committee Room had its Aircraft Recognition Charts, the outlines of the B-52, the A-40, the F-105; the weapon-identifications: "roccet," "bom," "na-pom." And when the arms-drills were signalled they were taken deadly seriously; there were no larks.

The Farming Co-operatives were five years old, and about 40 per cent of the peasants were involved, I was told—about 150 households per unit in the delta, fifty in the mountains. Every member claimed, naturally, to be unquestionably better off. But for a Vietnamese peasant to own a blanket and a mat and a mosquito net is to be well off.

In Hanoi virtually no private motor-traffic existed, but what did exist was, like all military transport, heavily camouflaged under piles of branches, palm-fronds, banana-leaves. Even in the towns this phenomenon continued, cars and lorries buried in greenery; Birnam Wood forever coming to Dunsinane.

The people, too—every citizen went for his military exercises with a cape of vegetation hanging about his shoulders. It was, perhaps, taken slightly to excess: the cult of camouflage had become in a way modish, and the new standard hat for everyone of importance was, paradoxically, a sort of topi of marked old-fashioned colonial appearance, garnished with little fronds of green cloth. The buses had rationalised the whole thing by being spray-painted in a formal pattern of foliage, like Oriental wallpaper.

Maybe the thing had become a little theatrical—but whom could it be supposed to impress, in a place that sees almost no strangers? This was a land where everyone considered it necessary to live in disguise, to inhabit their own country pretending they were not there, but invisible, resentfully. Rifles abounded in the most improbable places. There was a strong analogy of the early days of Israel, the same sense of wariness and never-ending siege.

You could call it what you liked, but it was a war, an enduring war and a special war, a dedicated and, within the limits of workable society, a complete one. There might be many arguments about its righteousness; they came as a rule from people ten thousand miles away. I just happened to be where few of the politicians or the soldiers or the statesmen who talked about North Vietnam had ever been—that is, in North Vietnam.

* * *

The fundamental technique of driving a car through Hanoi was evidently simple enough: the chauffeur set a course precisely down the middle of the street, with his foot on the gas and his hand on the horn. The only other required control was a casual hand on the steering wheel to ensure that the vehicle did not at any time stray an inch further than was necessary towards its proper side of the road.

There are probably fewer cars in Hanoi than in any city of comparable size, which is an extremely good thing. Occasionally, however, it did come to pass that two cars would approach one another in opposite directions, and this would give rise to a very tricky point of protocol. Since they were both in possession of the exact centre of the highway, which was the correct position and not to be readily surrendered, passengers in both cars were obliged to sustain a period of electric suspense, while the vehicles aimed at each other's radiators, with menacing blasts from the horn. Clearly there was a serious factor of chivalry involved, since among the small circle of Hanoi drivers it must have been held that he who first gave ground towards the side of the road would concede a point.

However, it was not considered that the national interest would be served by littering the streets with head-on collisions, and in consequence a compromise had been arrived at: when both cars were within inches of disaster there would come a simultaneous, barely perceptible swerve; nobody could actually be said to have retreated to the legal side of the road, but catastrophe was avoided.

Frequently, at this moment of alarming doubt, sitting there as the helpless part of a collision-course between two people who clung to a perilous position with inexorable obstinacy, there would flash through my mind the awesome analogy with the war that was going on all around.

The war was obsessive. Vast posters adjured, exhorted, encouraged, insisted. They resembled to the last item of oversimplified technique their counterparts in

China, that is to say they were crude without being particularly offensive—aesthetically, I mean; I suppose one could be in two minds about their content. Though even that, outside its melancholy context, might be held valid enough: the call to produce more rice, to make more textiles, to practise more Civil Defence, to be loyal to Uncle Ho.

Uncle Ho surveys the town in a hundred portraits—quizzical, faintly humorous, avuncular; he makes an agreeable change from the bloodhound solemnity of Mr Kosygin or the moon-faced blank of Chairman Mao. His very individual relationship with the people is symbolised in the odd honorific he has always insisted upon—not President Ho, nor Chairman Ho, nor even Father Ho, but *Bac Ho*: Uncle Ho, intimate but apart. The people respond by referring to him with a hint of friendly equivocation; it is not "Ho Chi Minh's Government," but "Uncle Ho *and* the Government," or "The Government says so, and so does Uncle Ho."

The rumours have long been rife all over Asia that the old President (he is rising seventy-six) is already past it, that his mind has lost its edge, that he is senile, that he has already been replaced, that he is produced to visitors only in occasional moments of lucidity. I can only say that when I saw him it must have been at such a moment, for his mind appeared both relaxed and acute, and his body looked fit as a fiddle. We shall arrive at that shortly.

Anyhow, the plaster casts of him which are on sale everywhere cost one dong eighty hao, while everyone else's (including, and indeed most prevalent, the late J. V. Stalin) cost only one fifty; a nice point of relative values.

Apart from busts of Uncle Ho and Uncle Joe there

was not a great deal to buy in Hanoi these days. The onset of Communist administrations seems over the world to cast a curious spell over all shops; not only do they have less to sell but they give an odd impression of not particularly wanting you to see what they have got; they exhibit a mood of shabby haphazardness that is highly discouraging. Not that Hanoi was ever the shopping Mecca of South-east Asia, but it did display a bit more than enamelled wash-basins and second-hand sparking-plugs. The Grand Magasin had turned into what they rather bewilderingly referred to as the State Department—that is, the state-run department store. It is extremely well-run, but dispiriting.

But the austerities of Hanoi life are well compensated for by the grace and good-humoured disposition of the people of Hanoi. The Vietnamese have always been loaded with charm; they come to terms with a poor and difficult life by moving through it with diffident and gentle courtesy. To walk around Hanoi was a sort of continual social pleasure. After the blank compulsive stares of India, the edgy resentful glances of Indonesia, there was something consolingly civilised about the casual acceptance of Vietnam. If they were interested, they looked; if they weren't, they didn't; when you caught an eye, it usually smiled. It is probably the case that nine out of ten Hanoiens, seeing the unusual sight of a strange longnose loose in their closed city, took me automatically to be a comrade-diplomat or a Soviet technician or a Fraternal Delegate; when they did learn who I was they were visibly taken aback, but their unshakeable good manners at once took control.

Occasionally it did go a little far: on sponsored visits to public places the most enthusiastic bystanders tended not only to greet the stranger, but actually to applaud him, under the perhaps understandable impression that any European permitted to roam around Hanoi these days must be acceptable, which is to say Communist. The practice became embarrassing after a while, since while there can be few more gratifying experiences than to be clapped by random strangers, there can equally be few more dispiriting reflections than to realise that it is being done under the impression that one is someone else.

It is also one of the interesting conventions of Eastern courtesy that anyone who is applauded must applaud back. For public figures, appearing on platforms to storms of clapping, this no doubt solves a problem: no need now for the deprecating gesture, the modest smile, the affected astonishment; important people in Hanoi appear in public applauding themselves like anything, and liking it.

But now the war had done something not known before, it had moved in and made itself manifest in Hanoi itself. The parks and gardens, and often the streets themselves, were scarred and disfigured with trenches and foxholes and the squat shapes of civilian air-raid shelters—they were little enough, to be sure, rows of half-buried emplacements built of brick and roofed with earth and tin; little more than hiding places. They sorted well with the bitter cult of camouflage.

This was by no means the case in the country, where the factor of concealment was of serious daily importance. But Hanoi had not itself been bombed, and continually it asked itself why. The Prime Minister, Pham Van Dong, told me that he had always expected that it would be, that he still expected that it would be. But the bridge over the immense Song Hong, the Red

River, still carried its confused streams of traffic, everything from railway-trains to buffalo-carts; its watch-towers are manned day and night, but it has not been attacked, as has almost every other bridge in the country. If it were attacked, that would constitute the real commitment, since it would almost certainly involve great loss of civilian life, and the little earthen hidey-holes will not help much.

In the evening there was little enough to do except to go to the Tea House by the lake. This must at one time have had a certain elegance, with its long narrow terrace overlooking the water. Now it had no elegance whatever, but it did have character, and it did do business. It was a People's Tea House, which is in no way in the sense used by the late Mr J. Lyons. It surged with people—workers, soldiers, militiamen, and girls. It is one of the conclusions of a mature and dedicated experience that on the whole the girls of Vietnam are perhaps the prettiest in the world, and unquestionably the most beguiling, being apparently incapable of an action or gesture that is not inherently sexy, while somehow maintaining a demeanour of virginal purity.

It was the great place for the family evening-out. All over the Orient the children tend to share in everybody's activities almost from the time they can walk, and in Vietnam they were especially all over the place, calm, self-possessed, and irresistible.

So the Tea House served its gallons of pale tea and its crates of pale beer to the screech and roar of a terrible loudspeaker system that blared out at random Vietnamese folk songs, Soviet martial airs, Peking opera, and archaic American boogie-woogie; so used were the discs and so antique the reproduction equipment it was hard to distinguish which was which.

Before nine the deal was over; the lights went out and the clientele went home, for tomorrow the city would start work, as always, at five in the morning.

* * *

I suppose the mind still groped around for Oriental glamour on the one hand and a reign of terror on the other, while the body continued its struggle with forms and oblique courtesies and requests. If the political fear were there, as doubtless it once had been, it had ceased to be apparent; it had also dissolved the glamour. These were the people of whom for many years one had known virtually nothing except from the special pleading of the zealots on both sides, the noisy and uncheckable overstatements. They gave a curious impression of normalcy. Somehow the North Vietnamese had escaped the uniform of the drab blue-cotton suit that in China is the badge of the new orthodoxy; so useful, so economic, so ideologically correct, and so dull. They had, however, adopted a spartan simplicity of shirt and trousers, for both men and women, and the high-buttoned tunic of faintly military cut for government servants. It seemed reasonable; one did not ask for embroidered silk in a revolutionary society, nor frills from a people starkly faced with the necessity of clothing itself somehow, and with small resources. Still, austerity had become a cult; it would be some time before a comrade showed up again in brocade, and so long as Uncle Ho chose to attire himself like a factory inspector so would his government, and his government's employees, and all those who wished to stand well with the government, which not unnaturally was everyone not personally in a mental home at the time.

The bans and barriers, the restrictions and inhibitions—they were there, to be sure, but not a few of them one had imported oneself. It is true that in Vietnam I sometimes felt that I had total and unfettered freedom to do and see anything whatever they wanted me to do—but some of that was prejudice. At no time did anyone attempt to interfere with my casual saunterings around Hanoi (though it was a very different matter indeed outside). They were deeply sensitive to photography and filming, however, partly on security grounds, which was understandable, but if anything rather more so on grounds that could only be defined as prestigious; they tended to steer the camera lens away from the seedier parts of town and grew restless in the presence of barefoot children and the ostentatiously poor. Pictures of such things, they said, would not be "useful." They would give the impression outside that North Vietnam was not a swinging, prosperous, up-to-date and progressive democracy, but a poor and backward country. When I suggested that it *was* a poor and backward country, despite its manifest advances, and that whatever sympathy existed in the world for its predicament and its courage derived exactly from that fact, they shook their heads sadly and said that this was not the image they wished to project. By and by, however, they became more flexible, when they began to realise that even Foreign Office guides could not wholly eliminate the backward and the shabby from the national scene, and that I did not interpret my function in North Vietnam as one of portraying it as a slum. This in any case would be untrue, because it is not.

The interpreters and *cicérones* assigned to me got off, at first, to an erratic start. The first was a young man of effervescent good nature and almost total uselessness; nobody could have been more well-meaning and few could have been more ineffectual. His impulse to please was in precisely inverse ratio to his powers of expression. On some principle difficult to follow someone had made the decision that he could speak English. It is indeed possible that he appreciated how to; it was just that he was incapable actually of *doing* it. Instead he had accumulated in his agreeable head all the many subsidiary clauses and turns-of-phrase and word-groups that are customarily used in English as meaningless and throat-clearing interludes—"I may say—" he would murmur, and come to a stop. "Ah, yes. But indeed. In fact. Nevertheless. I would suggest. It seems to me."

As a companion he might have been loyal and rewarding, but as an interpreter of the complex Hanoi scene he left too many imponderables, and he soon faded away. He was replaced by a very able and dedicated youngster (or whom I took to be a youngster, until I learned he was the contented father of two robust children) who was Mr Tien, and whose English was excellent and precise, and who was at all times eager to debate its more recondite usages. "Why do you lie *on* a bed, but sleep *in* a bed? Why do you go *to* bed? Why did you recently say: 'Well, I'm *for* bed?' What is 'good in bed'?"

It was an odd enough subject for his reflections, since bed was not a matter that could have been considered obsessive in Vietnam. There were to be times when I barely saw a bed for days on end. Even in the comparative tranquillity of Hanoi it was the practice to start one's programme, in conformity with local observances, at the crack of dawn; by a quarter to six every morning Mr Tien would be rapping discreetly on the bedroom door of the Unity Hotel, advising me that it was time to be about my business and visiting the textile mills or the Farming Co-operative or whatever it might be. On many occasions his dedication passed all bounds; he would knock me up in the grey half-light to say: "I have to inform you that we have no engagements today until noon."

Occasionally there were setbacks. "Not today." "So we aren't going to see the bicycle-factory after all?" And he would say: "Yes, yes!" Deep were the wearisome misunderstandings until one accepted the meaning of the Oriental positive-negative, which was: "Yes, you're right—we aren't going."

Superior to Mr Tien, and present on almost all occasions, was a vigorous and diverting official who appeared to be something in the National Films Board, and whose name was Mr Thing. That was indeed his name, and pronounced as spelt; for a time until I became adjusted to it it disconcerted me. It is not easy to form a proper relationship with someone called Mr Thing; to me there seemed a nuance of disparagement in addressing him at all.

Mr Thing was an addict to tea. He called himself (since his language was French) a "thé-iste," as he called me a "tabac-iste," and indeed an "alcool-iste," until the peculiar awfulness of the local *Lua Moi* vodka began to corrode even me, and drove me into a morose form of temperance. At every moment of leisure Mr Thing would produce from his pocket a packet of tea, and scrupulously concoct a potful of pallid brew. He had special tea for special occasions, and even for special places. "Le thé d'ici est mauvais," he would say. "J'apporte le mien; vous allez voir." It always tasted exactly the same to me, but I know nothing whatever about tea.

I would then be conducted to see people, generally in rooms that would seem never to have been used for any purpose other than interviews or conferences. The furniture was of the unresilient kind whose design found favour in the 'twenties; the table would be equipped with several newly opened packets of local cigarettes, which were very good, and the inevitable and apparently bottomless pot of tea. As in the Middle East the mark of professional success is the ability to consume endless very small cups of very black coffee, in the Orient it is the faculty to drink an infinity of cups of this very weak Chinese tea of which Mr Thing was so fond. The boundless supply of these was ensured by an article that was totally standard furnishing for every room I ever saw in Vietnam: the very large and most gaudily decorated vacuum-flask. These flasks linger in my mind, so much a part of Vietnamese life did they seem. The people are very proud of the fact that they are locally made, and extremely well made, too; as articles of beauty they had somewhat less appeal than their exotic painter probably imagined, but in the function of keeping water hot they were unsurpassed. From these, then, the teapot was refilled over and over again, with the result that by and by the tea itself, which had started its career weak enough, was soon indistinguishable from shaving-water.

One's host, the official or informant of whatever kind, would receive one with every evidence of sincere pleasure, which is more than one can say of similar encounters elsewhere, and, through the interpreter, invite questions.

When the question was asked the official would nod impassively, note it down, and wait. This was one of the eccentricities of ritual clearly borrowed from China, I had encountered it many times before: the questions were never answered as they were put; it was the practice to have all the questions put first, one after the other, and all the answers delivered in a string at the end. At first I had taken this to be an awful way of avoiding supplementaries, until I found they welcomed supplementaries just the same, only *they* too had to be grouped together in a bundle.

Then with the answers the words came: practised, fluent, hypnotic, Vietnamese, pausing for a moment here and there for translation, which itself was built, whatever the context, in phrases of time-worn familiarity. This was often a matter of linguistic limitation. In Vietnam the language trouble went a good deal deeper than tonal values. An Asian elusiveness, overlaid by the more familiar double-think, tended to make the simplest communications oblique. Too many officials spoke an English or French that did not make use of slogans but was actually *learned* in slogans: that is to say, the only word for "American" was "rabid-Imperialist-aggressor," as the only word for Vietnam was "heroic-valiant-resistance." The phrases were not used purely emotively; in a number of cases I actually believe that the official knew no other word for what he was intending to define. It gave a vapid tone to much conversation. I had been much exercised by this difficulty in China long before. In Chinese, which is a beautiful eccentric language, full of complex imagery, much of the worst banality was doubtless taken from these time-worn adages, and possibly the same can be said of Vietnamese. In the interpretations on which one had to depend one was brought to a condition of perhaps unjust exasperation. Familiar phrases assumed new meanings; the very words of which they were composed had standard and accepted applications. One never spoke of "Communism," but of "democracy"; one did not speak of "air raid," but of "tyrannical-assassination"; for Saigon soldiers (and I fear for the British too) one read "puppets"; for Hanoi one read "infallible." A "hero" was someone who had done a notably good day's work; a "saboteur" was someone who hadn't. For the truly contemptible were reserved epithets like "liberal," or "bourgeois." It had been a fairly familiar experience for me over the years, sojourning at intervals round the world in the comrades' countries; I could adjust without too much difficulty, but I confess to finding it tedious among a people otherwise sensitive to nuances.

However, it was probably no more inane than the opposing jargon of the other side, which spoke of "Commies" and "Reds" and "gooks" and "les jaunes" and so forth, with probably just as little examination of their own vocabulary. It was perhaps no sillier, but it was tiresome to find anything silly and inadequate in an ancient land that is, surely, among the unsilliest in the world. When they said to me: "Coming as you do from an Imperialist-colonialist-aggressor state . . ." they didn't really mean it; they just said it because they didn't know the other form of words. They were trying to mould something new and important out of the groping weariness of a poor country, and they were obliged to define it in the beaten-up old platitudes of a vanished age.

In Hanoi it seemed, as it had once done in China, that the affairs of state, especially in the lower echelons, were run by great numbers of able, agreeable, occasionally very clever men (and frequently women) of a certain age, which always appeared to be half one's own, all extremely neat and tidy and without exception wearing the standard People's Sandal made out of discarded automobile-tyres, and who looked upon me with much the same guarded surprise as I did upon them. They accorded me every courtesy, evinced a reasonable interest in what they clearly considered to be my totally incomprehensible job. They found it manifestly hard to understand how I could possibly be there, in these unprecedented circumstances, without *some* official sponsorship, some backing, some *arrière pensée*, some tricky and oblique motivation; when I assured them of the facts they would smile happily, but as a rule with patent disbelief. This in no way impeded their generosity and good manners.

They were helpful, within the terribly strict limitations placed upon their responsibility. They would present me with statistics and figures, which in general were percentages of a non-available base. This mattered remarkably little to me, since I grasp mathematical facts with all the accomplishment of a four-year-old child. There was no real point in the Co-operative chairman wrapping me up in graphs and garnishing them with seasonings of "subject as we are to unleashed vandalism" or "since we broke from the Imperialist yoke." These things I was ready to take for granted; I did not have to be sold on the wrongs of the system they had replaced, nor on the follies of the war that so oppressed us all. I did not have to be told of the amicable relationship between Vietnam and the selflessly generous governments of both China and the Soviet Union; this I could read in any of the thousands of dedicated handouts that seemed to constitute the entire production of the Foreign Languages Press. I had come so considerably to like the Vietnamese that I could from time to time have shouted at them for the fatuous way their spokesmen sometimes talk.

It is clear that a job like this produces a balance of the difficulties inherent in being, predictably, denounced elsewhere for the heresy of liking the North Vietnamese with the further risk of compromising the manifest facts. I have been doing this sort of thing long enough now not to care particularly about the first, but I have a certain concern about the second. It seemed to me undeniable that the new regime in Hanoi had produced a nation more united and, at least as far as I could judge, happier than before, and that I could discern no evidence at all that they were not, as they endlessly claimed, peace-loving. At the same time there was not the remotest doubt that no North Vietnamese individual had the slightest control over the policy or performance of his leaders, and that those leaders in their turn knew extremely little about the language of international persuasion, or even of international facts. It seemed to me highly probable that the real *responsables* of Hanoi knew every bit as little about the outer world they denounced in such embracing generalities as that outer world knew about them; not impossibly even less.

I knew so little about them; they knew so little about me. They had a hunger for reading, and so little to read. The big book-store in Hanoi was always crowded, but the choice was an alternative of pamphlets. The foreign section was pitiful: dog-eared treatises on amateur electronics and 1937 Guides to the Black Forest, relics of some old library liberated from a vanished diplomat or dispossessed old trader, queer memorials to other people's taste—the Bird Life of New Zealand, a Manual on Model Trains, Accountancy for Beginners, bits of Warwick Deeping.

The translations of foreign authors into Vietnamese read almost like a code—the works of Oan-ton Xcot (author of "Ai-van-ho"), of Dic-kenx, of Ho-no-le do Ban-xac, of Pux-kine, Le-nine, and Xta-line.

As for foreign newspapers, nobody ever heard of them. They must have come in somewhere, I suppose. I heard of no one who read them.

One of the results of this insulation was, it seemed to me, the dedicated over-evaluation of the protest-movements in both the United States and Europe. Hanoi regarded these as of the greatest importance. So indeed do I, but with perhaps a slightly different emphasis. In North Vietnam they were spoken of as though they heralded the hour before the dawn.

"But the whole democratically thinking faction of the Western world is behind us." Thus the argument, endlessly repeated. "There is Norman Morrison, who died for us. How can you deny him?"

It is part of the irony that I have here (as I would not have to do in Hanoi) to explain that Norman Morrison was the young American who publicly committed suicide by burning himself to death outside the Pentagon in Washington in November 1965 as a protest against the United States policies in Vietnam. It was a tragic, moving, stupid, honourable, useless thing to do. The news of its happening created a sensation in North Vietnam. The immolation of Norman Morrison was something so electrifying to the Vietnamese, a gesture so completely in accord with their own sense of the dramatic, that while I was there, weeks after his death, they were still calling meetings in his honour; his picture was exhibited on a dozen billboards, his name—"No-man Mo-li-sonh"—was venerated in print; he was virtually canonised; he had gone into North Vietnamese mythology. They even had a song about him: "No-man Mo-li-sonh Cong Song Mai"—Norman Morrison Shall Never Die." How does one answer that?

I wrote about this phenomenon later in the newspapers; I spoke of it on American television. And when I turned up in New York shortly after my return the first question I was asked by a well-read and well-informed political journalist of my acquaintance was: "What nobody gets here is, who is the man Morrison you talk about?" In his homeland, clearly, his horrible death had made no impact whatever; already he was forgotten.

But not in Hanoi. In the public parks were picture-exhibitions with photographs of protest-meetings in Berkeley, in London, in Sofia, in Paris. "Now, at least, the Americans will understand!"

"It is possible you exaggerate the political power these things have; admirable as they may be, they are not yet effective."

"But there is more than that; there is your Bertrand Russell. How can you deny these people?"

I was not denying them. I was trying to explain them. But how? That Norman Morrison did not become the Joan of Arc of American liberalism? They did not really believe me when I said that Bertrand Russell is not yet the surging dynamic behind an effective British opposition. While I was in Hanoi there was a very considerable public demonstration for, as the banners proclaimed: "The good and peace-loving people of the United States"—a paradox so startling that I would not have credited it, had many of the placards not been in English. Demonstrations! Today we can demonstrate in favour of demonstrations.

Perhaps the enduring memory of Vietnam will be that curious alternation of hope and despair. The happiness came from the commonplace: the masses of enchanting and clearly beloved children, the impulsive friendship for strangers, the simple fact that everybody somehow *looked* in a way redeemed. The weariness came from the emphasis on all the peripheral aspects of Communism—the impenetrable platitudes, the badges on people's tunics, the stage-management of happenings that might well have happened anyhow, the evasiveness—the disappearance of those old restaurants and clubs; no one knew where anything was in case it might have a reactionary connotation; you couldn't use the telephone without your guide. You knew they were good, and they forced pamphlets on you saying they were perfect. You wanted to protest: "Please be happy and well-clad and love your babies as you clearly do, and your country as you clearly do, and be brave in adversity as you clearly are, and I am surely on your side. But pray do not tell me that every citizen is prosperous when that is not the case, do not tell me you have eliminated need when you have not, do not insist that you have shot down nine hundred

American bombers with rifle-fire; please ask me to like you as people and not as angels. I am frank with you; be frank with me."

But there was no reason why they should be; in the circumstances I am not sure I blame them; it was their suffering, not mine.

LAND OF THE BROKEN BRIDGES

THROUGH THE HOURS of daylight practically nothing whatever moved on four wheels on the roads of North Vietnam: hardly a car or a truck; from the air, in the sunlight, it must have looked as though the country had no wheeled transport at all. That, of course, was the idea. It was the roads and the bridges that were being bombed; it was held to be no longer safe, after sunrise, to be near either. Furthermore it was the illusion that was important; there was a kind of aesthetic importance in creating illusions, and there were, of course, two. One was that the North of Vietnam is a growing and progressive industrial nation. The other was that, between sunrise and sunset, it was inhabited by nobody at all.

In the paddy-fields in the sunlight the farmers were reaping their third harvest of the year, which had been especially abundant. I know nothing of the craft, but it seemed to me odd, in that here one could see every successive process of agriculture in train at the same time: within a mile people were ploughing the fields, sowing the seed, reaping the crop and threshing the harvest. They moved among the rice with their sickles —snick, snick, grasp; snick, hold and turn over; snick and fold; the wonderfully economical and accomplished peasant movement; what would a time-and-motion operator make of this? They moved among the rice bowed under a shawl of foliage, the camouflage that gave everyone a kind of carnival air, like so many Jack-o'-the-Greens. At the corners of every field stood what looked like sheaves of iron corn, and which were stacks of rifles. The roads stretched long and empty, leading from nowhere to nowhere. One could have taken it for a charade; in this land does *nothing* travel from place to place?

Then the sun went down, and everything started to move.

At dusk the roads became alive. From a thousand arbours and copses and the shelter of trees the traffic materialised; the engines were started and the convoys emerged from invisibility, began to grind away through the darkness behind the pinpoints of masked head-lights. There were miles of them—heavy Russian-built lorries, anti-aircraft batteries of guns, all deeply buried under layers of branches and leaves; processions of huge green haystacks. By day North Vietnam is abandoned; by night it thuds and groans with movement. It was an excessively fatiguing routine for those of us who were trying to capture this peculiar picture: moving always by night, and working always by day.

In this fashion I drove down to what is called the "fighting area" in the central province of Thanh Hoa.

It is not a "fighting area" at all, in the sense that every province of South Vietnam is a "fighting area"; in North Vietnam no battles take place, no guerillas resist, no American soldiers aggress; north of the 17th Parallel there is no ground-bound war. This is merely the neighbourhood most vulnerable, and most attacked, by the air-raiders.

It was far from easy to get permission to go. Permits were held back—and I imagine reasonably—simply because it was held to be an unsafe part of the country, and nobody was particularly anxious to have me killed. I cannot for a moment imagine that anyone in North Vietnam would have felt personally bereaved at my disappearance, but I can understand that to have observed this dubious Westerner going to his maker under a stick of American high-explosive would, at this juncture, have been an embarrassment—not without its own especial ironies, but a confounded nuisance. Repeatedly I was asked to appreciate the importance of their responsibility. It seemed to me most excessive. The manager of the hotel in Hanoi, who was very small but one of the most bloodthirsty men I ever met, kept darting forth and saying: "Now you will understand the truth. Now you will see for yourself. Whomh, whomh—then you will know. Try some suffering, monsieur; how splendid."

I thought of saying that I had probably had a good deal more whomh, whomh in my life than he had in his, and from a greater variety of sources, since for a number of years that had been my imbecile trade, but it seemed to serve little purpose. I was in any case dependent on this ebullient little patriot to supply me with enough food to last me the journey.

So in this fashion I drove down to the "fighting area," in the central province of Thanh Hoa. How many nights I was to spend in this way, bouncing around in a Russian jeep, buried in ironclad technical luggage, my knees overlain by Mr Thing, praying for the dawn.

It was a landscape of almost wildly theatrical beauty. The moon was full. We cleared the city checkpoint—no one leaves Hanoi by road without a clearance—and rumbled down through the Vietnamese countryside which, in certain conditions, is wholly bizarre. It is a plain studded with strange little precipitous mountains, as though a shower of enormous meteorites had become embedded in the land; it is a geological phenomenon I do not understand; once before I had seen it, in the South Chinese province of Kwangsi; in the light of the full moon it is eerie beyond expression; it is like living in the heart of a seventeenth-century Oriental water-colour.

Two hours out of Hanoi we were stopped; all the convoys were halted. Everybody got out and smoked cigarettes, and relaxed on the little stacks of rice-straw that had been left to dry beside the road. A couple of hours earlier there had been a raid, a clean hit on the highway, and the road was for the time being impassable. It was, they said, happening all the time.

By and by we got on the move again; by the time we inched through the darkness to the bombed area it seemed it was already passable, though only with difficulty. It was hard to see in the darkness what was happening—though later, after many such experiences, I came to know: great multitudes of women had somehow been recruited or accumulated from the neighbourhood and were filling in the holes and reconstituting some sort of a surface for the road, out of the piles of stones and gravel that were permanently kept by the roadside, I assume for just this purpose. It was impossible to count the number of women, but there were several hundred. This, they said, happened frequently; almost every major road in the country was in a semi-permanent condition of running repair.

Two main bridges on the road ahead were gone long since; they had been destroyed in the early raids; they had been replaced with pontoons of bamboo rafts. Usually the replacement was a ferry; North Vietnam is a wilderness of ferries in the delta region; they take up a tremendous proportion of travelling time. Some were manipulated by a motor-launch that nudged them across from alongside; some were manhandled over by crews of men pulling them over by a fixed cable. For anyone obliged to drive much through the nights of the Red River delta they were a terrible bore. Sometimes a pontoon-bridge was alternated with a ferry, to cause confusion among the American reconnaisance aircraft. Frequently with the makeshift bridges, when daylight came and traffic stopped, one end of the floating bridge was detached, so that the whole structure could drift down and lie parallel with the bank, and become invisible. There never was a place where such importance was attached to invisibility.

But the great showplace of the province of Thanh Hoa was the famous Ham Rong bridge. This, too, has almost become part of the folklore of Vietnam. It was not an especially impressive bridge, though it carried a road and a railway, but it had become a dedicated object of American attention. It had been attacked—they said, when I got there—more than a hundred times, by at least a thousand aircraft. It was scarred and pitted and twisted; its girders were deeply burned and marked, and the area around it was in a terrible mess, but the bridge endured, and still carried both the road and the railroad. It lay in a kind of ravine between two very steep little hills; it was probably extremely hard to hit; it would require a very steep, oblique, and difficult bombing-approach.

It was my impression, and I am not wholly ignorant of the processes of tactical bombing, that the United States attacks on North Vietnam had been, as they claimed, aimed generally at what they could define as military objectives—that is to say, bridges and roads.

Whether a great power can claim justification for the arbitrary blowing up of the bridges and roads of an alien state against whom they have not invoked the civility of even declaring war is a separate question. It is no particular secret that I, personally, am vehemently and explicitly against the whole thing; I am obliged to insist that I am vigorously opposed to anybody bombing anybody, but especially against this, which seems to me to be as wanton as it is useless; both militarily silly and individually cruel. At the same time it is fatuous to define the United States assault on North Vietnam as "terror bombing"; the strikes have been against objects that I suppose some obtuse and pedantic commander could define as legitimate, in his limited sense. The difficulty is, with a society that did not build itself in the image of a fortress, that people tend to accrete and establish themselves in the neighbourhoods of roads and bridges, for reasons of convenience, and that in consequence their habitations tend to suffer when such things are bombed, especially when they are bombed by operators who are not only rather poor shots, but have no particular reason to care about the secondary effects of their performance, and who may reason that in a place like Vietnam any moderately substantial building must have some military function.

I do not believe that the Americans set out to bomb homes and hospitals; if they had wished to do so it would have been extremely easy to do so. Nevertheless it is a fact that homes and hospitals have been destroyed by their bombs. I do not think the strategic thinkers of the United States Air Force intended to wage war on the peasants of North Vietnam; nevertheless they managed to kill quite a few.

The *New York Times* estimated that in the ten

months before my visit more than 18,000 bombing sorties had been flown against the North—an average of about sixty a day—with a total of some 36,000 tons of bombs. The North Vietnam estimate is a great deal higher.

In the vicinity of the Ham Rong bridge was the only bombed hospital I saw: a tuberculosis clinic that had taken a loose stick of bombs on both sides; it was blasted and deserted. Its equipment had been taken away, or such of it as was worth taking away; a group of old men were desultorily salvaging beams and panels that looked as though they might be of use elsewhere. The houses of the village beside it were shells, deserted.

In the nearby co-operative of Xoan Hanh the villagers, threshing the rice with very mediaeval-looking flails beside a stacked pile of modern Czech automatic rifles, recalled that the hospital had gone three months earlier. They were not especially dramatic about it; there had been only three casualties, they said; it was largely an out-patient clinic. Why, I asked, had not something been done about repairing it? The neighbourhood, they replied, was raided so frequently it would hardly be worth it; instead the institution had been rebuilt miles away, they had no idea where.

The province of Thanh Hoa is the biggest in the north of Vietnam—it has about ten thousand square kilometres, and a population of two million. It is described as the first line of resistance for the North, and the rear of the revolution of the National Liberation Front.

"Is there much interchange of people? Do you get southerners crossing up here; do you send men down there?"

"Not much through here. We understand most of

that traffic goes down the western border. But like everyone else in North Vietnam, many of us have relatives in the South, and the other way round; there are thousands of relatives who have never managed to see each other for ten years."

Since the "escalation" Thanh Hoa has been the province that has been worst hit of all in the North. They claimed to have logged more than four hundred United States sorties, involving about fifteen hundred aircraft. They also claimed to have shot down just rather more than a hundred; this was of course uncheckable.

There was a rather curious *façon de vivre* in Thanh Hoa, involving a daily removal. We arrived in the hours of darkness, as one can do no other in the peculiar circumstances of contemporary North Vietnam transport, and were bedded in what seemed a quite new if rather austere State Guest House. At dawn we were obliged, as they called it, to "evacuate" it. It was held to be unsafe by daylight; it was too near the celebrated bridge. We then drove a dozen miles or so and set up headquarters in another, smaller, infinitely tattier and more engaging establishment, a four-roomed thatched bungalow with no amenities whatsoever but with a great deal of broken-down charm. Its thatch was inhabited by great numbers of bats, who emerged at dusk in whirling squadrons. The night air crepitated to the sound of cicada, the anthem of South-east Asia. To some this noise, like the sound of an unstoppable sewing-machine, is tiresome and exasperating; I find it the most soothing sound on earth.

But we still had to return to establishment number one to take our bath; huge pans of boiling water ladled into tubs in unlit bathrooms; there is an interesting sensual satisfaction in bathing in the darkness which may repay further experimentation.

This was the first opportunity I had had of seeing the countryside by daylight. How much more attractive is all of South-east Asia outside its towns! Here was the Far East of the conventional imagination, of the scroll paintings and the silken screens; a composition of waters and mountainsides and mists, curious trees and amber lighting; in some inexplicable way at the same time both empty and vitally inhabited.

I think most Westerners have some difficulty in really comprehending the extraordinary intensity of effort necessary even for subsistence in many of these Asian lands, where for so long a man could be tipped over almost to starvation by some quite marginal circumstance—by a poor harvest, by a rain failure, by the caprice of his local taxation officer, even by the hazard of a funeral or a wedding, and the ensuing load of debt. Work was so exhaustingly hard it left little energy to spill over into politics, and government, local or colonial, had been something remote, a factor to be avoided by every stratagem, especially at times of tax collection and war.

How odd that one should have invented the myth that the Asians are fatalists, that they are "passive"—the Asians who live in a land so incessantly exacting, where a man must wield a scoop all day to irrigate his fields, that must be forever preserved from attack and nourished with the products of his own body, that demands every sort of quality *except* fatalism.

Here were the villages, and the mud bricks drying in the sun—the villages that grew out of the land, were made from the land, that crumbled back into the land to make more bricks for more villages; the endless cycle that had little enough to do with the "state of war."

But each one had its little earthen strongpoint, its foxholes, its stack of rifles. You could not escape anything anywhere.

In the village of Nanh Ngang, hard by the famous bridge, I was presented to Miss Nguyen Thi Hanh, who was famous, they said, in song and story. Miss Hanh was a quite attractive twenty-eight-year-old, with the indefinable air of resolution and authority that in other climes marks out the Girl Guide leader or the Captain of Games. She was offered as a Labour Hero and a People's Hero, and wore small decorations to prove it. She was clearly adjusted to a measure of local celebrity as the local Resistance pin-up. She had once been on a delegation to Moscow. Pictures of her from several patriotic magazines decorated the walls of her very simple, austere, and impeccably tidy room.

The point about Miss Hanh was that she was the commander of the local militia. In order to dispel any impression that she was a Boadicea, however, she began on our arrival to go through a sequence of activities that were unmistakably feminine: she poured tea with grace and skill, she combed her hair; at one moment she even produced a doll and played with it, in a somewhat off-hand way. I gained the impression, from the casual skill with which she adjusted her attitude to the camera, holding the gesture for exactly the right moment, and the accomplished manner in which she delivered her lines on cue, that she was not wholly unfamiliar with the experience of being Exhibit A of the province of Thanh Hoa. As it subsequently turned out, there has been scarce a foreign visitor to these parts of North Vietnam who has not had the opportunity of meeting Miss Hanh.

Miss Hanh admitted she had been a volunteer for some time; her ambition had always been to dedicate herself to the people's welfare and the defence of the nation, because President Ho had this very much at heart and therefore, she felt, so should she. It seemed an unexceptional sentiment.

By and by we moved outside to the riverside, and Miss Hanh obligingly put her women's corps of the militia through their paces. I was in time to grow rather familiar with these "mock fights," as they were called —the air-raid drills and rehearsals that had become embodied in the North Vietnam way of life. They were called regularly, or impromptu; there was no doubt at all that this routine did in fact keep the people both in the city factories and in the country very much on the alert.

Miss Hanh's demonstration was less persuasive than many—a covey of pretty little girls dressed in leaves popping into foxholes and pointing their rifles at the sky, with Miss Hanh gesturing dramatically upwards, exactly as in her many photographs.

She also had a little model aircraft carved from wood, about a foot long, which was brandished through the air at the end of a long pole, while everybody aimed their empty guns at it. (This may in fact be a tactic of anti-aircraft training that is of greater usefulness than it appears to be; at first I thought Miss Hanh's property toy bomber was a piece of rather nonsensical stagecraft, until I saw variations of this model-device being put to use all over the place. The Vietnamese are not usually given to fooling themselves over something so elementary.)

It all seemed so palpably make-believe, however—the vital great steel bridge defended by a chorus of pretty little girls; I felt awkward and rueful. One said: "Yes, very nice; well done, ladies," as though it had been a folk-dance contest.

And then—very suddenly, as I was walking back broodily from the riverside to the village—the alarm went in all truth, with a thumping of a great barrel-drum somewhere, and the war-game was real after all, with the sighing howl of the jets overhead, the thud of anti-aircraft fire from somewhere around and, for all I know, a tiny volley from Miss Hanh's young ladies in the foxholes.

But on this occasion the planes were not after us, but streaking homewards south from some unknown enterprise in the interior. For a while the high air ached with the bitter whine of the engines, but there is a special tenor, hard to define, that marks the sound of bombers that have one's own position in mind and those that are high-tailing it back for the base. The village took cover philosophically, but by the time the children had been herded into the earth dugouts the flight was doubtless far away.

There were several such alerts while I moved around the country, and it is fair to try to analyse one's reaction. It is not easy. The first, obviously, was simple interest—in watching the manner in which the children materialised from nowhere in small crocodiles, and were shepherded into the dugouts; the tension that gripped everyone in a visible moment of truth: the hands that shot out to indicate the position of the planes, the bubble of excited chatter that would spontaneously burst at the same moment from every watching group, the dead silence when it seemed an attacking run was on and the bombs might fall, the low-pitched communal sigh when it was all over, a relaxation that was almost palpable.

Then what supervened, I think, was not the emotion of fear (for I was at no time in any particular danger, except from accident) nor was it high-minded horror at this intolerable breach of the rule of law. There was somehow a sense of outrage against civility; what an impertinence, one felt, what arrogance, what an offence against manners, if nothing else; by what right do these airmen intrude over a country they do not recognise, with which they are not formally at war; who gave these people the sanction to drop their bombs and rockets on other people's roads and bridges and houses, to blow up the harvest, to destroy people of whom they know absolutely nothing?

The crews up there were almost certainly decent American young men, but from down below one felt of their behaviour as not so much wicked, or tyrannical; but as wholly insolent, and in its way futile. These people in Vietnam were hardly angelic; in many cases they were troublesome, unmanageable, awkward; but they were friendly and shy people, and very poor; any pilot up there made more in a week than most of these people did in a year. Would this sort of thing blow Communism out of their heads?

Apart from the cadres and the politicians, who indeed could be truculent and demanding, most of these people never wanted anything in their lives but to be let alone, to get on with their lives, which have always been hard, to see that the crop was got in and the children got enough to eat. From down below, the raids seemed not so much a "rabid Imperialist aggression," but just a crude and inexcusable imposition, a vulgar demonstration of the strong against the weak.

One thing already appeared to be sure: if the bombing of North Vietnam had been designed either to terrorise the people into submission or to crush their economy into ruin, its effect on both counts seemed to me precisely the reverse.

So far from terrorising and disrupting the people the bombings seemed to me to have stimulated and consolidated them. By the nature of the attacks so far, civilian casualties had not been very great, but they had been great enough to provide the government of the Vietnam Republic with the most totally unchallangeable propaganda they could ever have dreamed of. A nation of peasants and manual workers who might have felt restive or dissatisfied under the stress of totalitarian conditions had been obliged to forget all their differences in the common sense of resistance and self-defence. From the moment the United States dropped its first bomb on the North of Vietnam, she welded the nation together unshakeably. Every bomb since was a bonus for Ho Chi Minh.

Nor is this an economy that can be easily wrecked by high-explosive. This was a peasant, agrarian society; immensely resilient. The Pentagon's thought-processes seemed to me considerably those of a highly developed and sophisticated Western society; even in their own interests the US planners failed to recognise the realities of a society like this. A bomb here, a bomb there; a family eliminated here or there; a rice-field churned into swamp—these were troublesome, infuriating; they were not disabling.

The destruction of a bridge or a road—in Western terms it could be disastrous. Here, it was a nuisance.

The people would mend it, or they would go some other way. When I drove to Haiphong it took three hours along the country's most important road. While I was away the road was cut. It took seven hours to return—but we returned; in Vietnam there is always another way.

If the day came when the industries were bombed and destroyed, it would be a grievous setback to a nation that is only just beginning to grope among the problems and advantages of industry—but it would make, fundamentally, very little difference to them. Every single industrial enterprise in the country could be ruined—and it would directly affect about 5 per cent of the working population. Vietnam is not Detroit, nor even Washington or London. Its people can survive the inconveniences of destruction, dismay, and death. They have learned how, over twenty-five years.

I fear we have learned less.

VISIT TO A CEMETERY

From Thanh Hoa we set off north again—as ever, only at the disappearance of the sun—aiming in the general direction of Hanoi. It was a journey of more than usual confusion, because when we reached the town of Ninh Dinh, we stopped, and for no reason made immediately clear we all were taken into what must at one time have been the Mairie: clearly a building of some municipal government purpose, full of gaunt halls and reception-rooms. In one such room we were deposited, while everybody went somewhere else and consulted, in a mood of almost palpable disquiet. Only too often have I experienced this situation, when in the middle of an adequately well-organised occasion something unforeseen has suddenly cropped up for which no automatic response is available, and for which no improvisation is permissible. In such circumstances, it has been my experience, the Establishment solidifies, takes its own counsel, consults it own oracles; it is idle to ask either what is the cause of the trouble or its potential solution, because this would be doing the one unthinkable thing, which is involving the *subject* of the occasion—to wit, oneself—with the difficulty, since that would be conceding that occasionally things go wrong. It is one of the exasperating—and yet, in human terms, somehow endearing—considerations of working in totalitarian societies that one must accept the convention that things never go wrong *administra-*

tively; one must always blame an earthquake or an act of what can only be called non-God; there must never be any executive fault.

In this case the trouble was simplicity itself: a few hours before the American aircraft had come over and smashed up the road over which we were supposed to pass. That was hardly an exceptional circumstance; it was happening all the time. On this occasion, however, it appeared to have assumed a mysteriously great importance. Our men returned from their conclave with very solemn faces to say: they were sorry, but the programme was off; there was nothing for it but that we return to Hanoi. Perhaps later we could return to see what we had been organised to see, but tonight—no, better return.

At this point a curious reaction came to pass, possibly only realisable in conditions of acute stress. Normally, and for obvious reasons, one argued about practically nothing; one accepted one's orders and did what one was told; in a conflict of determinations it was manifest who would win; in consequence there was as a rule no dispute. On this occasion, however, for some reason or other, I began to feel an obsessive sense of injustice, and furthermore of folly. To return to Hanoi now would mean another three or four hours of jolting in the jeep, the crossing of at least another two or three ferries; to return—as they suggested—would entail exactly the same thing; whereas at this moment we were within half an hour of our objective, give or take another American raid. It was three o'clock in the morning; I was almost anaesthetised with fatigue. I refused to move.

The effect was most unusual. Everybody retired for another conclave in the back room. I made my decision manifest by making myself up a makeshift bed on an assortment of chairs, and composing myself ostentatiously for sleep. The *responsables* were obviously on the wire to Hanoi—not the easiest of operations, I imagine, at any time, and certainly a big business at this time in the morning.

By and by they returned, and with the great courtesy that marks every transaction among Vietnamese, however personally infuriated they may feel, it was intimated that although the accepted road to our destination had in fact been destroyed, we could, come daylight, find another.

The great business now was to find somewhere to sleep for the remainder of the night, since for some recondite reason we could no longer remain in the place where we were. "People do not sleep here," they said; which was a remark that, even in my condition of total exhaustion, I could understand. Nobody, given any alternative, would willingly sleep in the town hall of Ninh Dinh.

The difficulty was to find anywhere else. For what seemed to be forever, but was probably an hour, we jolted around in the jeep. I had long ago lost interest in the proceedings, and crouched in the back seat surrendered to dreams of happier things. I was shaken into wakefulness to find myself outside a house—a farmer's house; that is to say a simple room over which there was a roof and in which there was a bed. The bed was a four-legged structure on which were nailed boards; nothing else. I lay down on it; the cold was so intense that I began to shiver to the degree that the bed began actually to *rattle*; such an experience has never come my way before. Out of kindness, or perhaps to ensure an hour's peace, the Vietnamese lady of the house shortly appeared, and threw over me a blanket. The blanket was of the weight and consistency of a normal European daily newspaper, but it consoled me to the extent that I fell abruptly into a profound sleep, from which I was loudly aroused exactly half an hour later, at the accepted hour of five a.m. Considerable numbers of delightful Vietnamese children appeared from all directions, saluting my extraordinary presence and giving me good day. I stumbled to my feet, numbed with cold and exhaustion, and wished them well. This was my eleventh night without repose. I began to feel as though I had no top to my head at all.

Within an hour we were at the famous Aircraft Cemetery of North Vietnam. This has achieved something of the circumstances of a national shrine. It became clear when, before entering the park, we were asked to sign a Visitors' Book. Where Visitors' Books exist, I argue, spontaneity ceases; this is not to say that actuality comes to an end, only that the truth is being moulded to a purpose. That is not to say that it ceases to be a truth.

In this place, which is a valley below a ridge of poignantly lovely hills, beside a very ancient temple that was in the old Resistance days a guerilla headquarters, they have gathered together a great multitude of the bits and pieces of American aircraft that the Vietnamese claim to have destroyed over North Vietnam, since the war was "escalated" over their own territory. It consists of a series of piles of mechanical debris —since inevitably a modern aircraft of tremendous potential, if destroyed in the air, descends in a miscellany of bits and pieces most of which are no bigger than a tablecloth. However, they had all been labelled by name—the name of the aircraft and, since it is the custom of the United States aviators to identify themselves with their machines by printing their own names on the fuselage—the name of the pilot too. One had no means of knowing what had happened to him. It was all increasingly sad.

There must have been, in this strange place, about thirty such "carcases," as they call them, on display. Similar "cemeteries" exist all over the country. It is impossible, without a tremendous collusion of computers both in Hanoi and in Washington, to know what it means. I know merely this: that in the centre of Hanoi is displayed a scoreboard—one can call it nothing else—on which is noted, every day, the total of American bombers claimed to have been shot down over North Vietnam, and that when I left, before Christmas of 1965, the total claimed was 915.

This is either wild, or mad, or true—how can I know? The United States, at that moment, had admitted a loss of aircraft shot down of 216. The disparity of claims to admissions is too great to be accounted for in mathematical error. I am obliged to record the simple fact: the Vietnamese claim to have destroyed nearly a thousand American aircraft. If this is the case, it is about four times the success the RAF had in the Battle of Britain in the early 1940s. I attest to nothing; the two places whose secrets I cannot claim to know are Hanoi and the Pentagon, but this I can say: on that chilly morning in Ninh Dinh I saw a lot of fragments of only too expensive American Air Force machinery which had never got home, the debris of technology that had cost many men their lives, and the only thing I could say, as I have said all my life, is: what a sad and silly waste.

THE SOLDIER FROM THE SOUTH

IT WAS ENDLESSLY and formally insisted in Hanoi that the Republic of Vietnam, North and South alike, is one state, temporarily divided at the 17th Parallel, and that this fact is acknowledged in the Geneva Agreement of 1954, which was accepted and signed by Britain, France, Vietnam, Laos and Cambodia. The implementation of this legal fact is what, they say, the war is all about. Only the United States impedes it, by force of arms.

The United States equally argues that if this unified state comes about, by the elections required by Geneva, Vietnam will become a Communist country overnight. This is almost certainly true.

The Vietnamese case is, I would say, unanswerable legally, but they were in great need of someone to put it plausibly. What was taking place in Vietnam, both South and North, was an offence to international decency both disgusting and absurd, and one of its chiefest wrongs was that it is corrupting both the assailants and victims alike.

However, what was quite clear in this lunar landscape of North Vietnam was that the people had a totally unshakeable determination to win the war, on their terms. Not to make an end of it, or find a way out of it, or "conclude an agreement" about it. They had the extraordinary and rather impressive nerve to insist upon winning it.

Victory, however, had a strict definition, which is the implementation of the Geneva Agreement of 1954, which requires a Vietnam united under popular elections, and the elimination of all foreign troops from both South and North. To Hanoi, winning the war did not mean the crushing or destruction of US forces, it meant their departure. This they would achieve, they said, if it took forever.

The thing is militarily illogical—a poor and small Asian country convinced it can successfully challenge the richest and strongest nation on earth—but the mood was extremely pervasive. It is a fact that they claimed to reject the machinery of compromise categorically. Indeed the word "negotiation" had become an emotive, even offensive word, in the way words these days acquire unreasonable connotations, as "appeasement" did in the 'forties, as "peace" did in the 'fifties. "Negotiation" to Hanoi merely meant some devious stratagem to get the US off the hook, to rescue her from a cruel and intolerable situation.

"The negotiations are over," they repeated. "The negotiations were concluded in 1954, at Geneva, by international signature. There is no more to say—except when they shall be made good."

It is nevertheless true to say that Hanoi now seemed to require something more than that; it wanted to see the US chastised for her behaviour in the way especially punitive in Oriental eyes: by shame, by loss of face. It was not pleasant, but when you saw what had been done to this place it is at least comprehensible.

The painful thing is that this attitude, this emotion, is strangely foreign to the accepted normal character of the Vietnamese. The photographs one saw from the South, the stories one read of Vietnamese barbarity to their countrymen, their disregard for human pain (those terrible spiked mantraps, the routine acceptance of torture) are in some tormented way a charade of our times. If this bloody war had done no worse, it could be condemned for corrupting a quiet and tranquil Asian atmosphere into a contest of beastliness, and it should not have happened here.

I hasten to say this is not brainwashing. I have known the South-east Asians for twenty years, and I might well wish Vietnam had found another road than Communism. But I would argue that is their affair. Many may disagree.

I think it is a fact that on the whole the Western industrial societies have a very imperfect notion of the nature of Asian Communism, for which there really should be another and less emotive word. It is a specially local product of a peasant economy, the most obvious factor of which is that it caters, for the first time, for hopes as well as for needs. I should guess that you would have to look a long way in Vietnam, outside official cadres, for a truly doctrinaire Marxist. But everyone trusted Uncle Ho.

* * *

I talked for an hour with a lieutenant-colonel in the Vietnam regular Army in Hanoi, whose name was not insisted upon since his function was head of liaison with the National Liberation Front of South Vietnam, elsewhere known as Viet Cong. His headquarters, with a nice irony, was in a villa of surpassing ugliness that had formerly been the property of Madame Nhu, the "dragon lady" who might be half-forgotten in the West but who was remembered with a special loathing in Hanoi.

"This war is often described as one which nobody can win," he said. "You have used the phrase yourself. I would dispute that. It can be won, in the sense that our objective can be attained. That is, as you know, no more—but certainly no less—than the implementation of the Geneva Agreement. That entails the withdrawal of American troops. When it comes about, it will constitute what our government will regard as victory. We require nothing more of the Americans than that they go home.

"The fighting in the South will inevitably grow fiercer and more bloody, and I do not by any means reject the possibility of its escalating far more directly in the North. In a word, the war is going to get far worse. But Mr Macnamara has miscalculated in several important ways.

"It is argued that for regular forces to cope with guerillas requires a proportion of five to one. If you assess the Liberation Front as about 180,000, which is more or less correct at this moment, that would need the best part of a million men. Yet Mr Macnamara reckons he can turn the tide with about 200,000 American troops and 500,000 puppets." (In the accepted vocabulary of the situation "puppet" means South Vietnamese troops.)

"Furthermore the guerilla forces are also increasing, and very fast. This is of course not difficult, as already most of the South has been liberated. On the accepted proportion, the Americans would soon need about two million men in the field, which is preposterous.

"This is not to take into account the difference of fighting spirit. Our people know what they are fighting for, which is simply their homeland. The American boys do not. I don't blame them; it must be extremely hard to die for a concept that just says 'anti-Communism,' especially when it must be obvious to the intelligent ones that by no means all the Liberation soldiers are Communist at all. Of course the leadership is Communist, and we who sustain their struggle are Communist, but we could hardly require party allegiance from people who only want to be patriots.

"The nature of the fighting in the South has greatly changed. It is becoming inaccurate to refer to 'guerillas.' What is happening now is that the Liberation people are meeting the enemy in genuine battles on a conventional pattern—Phei Me, Van Tuong, Do Bac and so on are examples.

"Naturally the United States forces have an enormous superiority in weapons and equipment; in no circumstances could we ever begin to match them in resources. But in the new phase of the struggle we, that is to say the Liberation forces, are putting a strong emphasis on what we in our language call 'catch-and-grasp'—hand-to-hand fighting, you would say. It is fair to say that in this sort of thing the Americans can always be defeated—they dislike it, and they are untrained for it. It is intensely disagreeable, and you have to have a particularly good reason to be able to do it at all.

"Another miscalculation of Mr Macnamara has been his reliance on his superiority in fire-power; he put too much trust in the effect of the B-52 bombers. It is true that for some time they had a very destructive effect on the Liberation soldiers, but they learned how to cope with them.

"It is a question of effective sheltering. The Liberation people have become extremely skilled at the business of deep shelters. They have clearly no means of opposing the bombers in fire-power, therefore it is necessary to survive it, wait until it is over, and return at once to the attack. There is a great emphasis on the practice of scattering and concealment and swift re-groupment. In this it is even an advantage to be short of mechanical transport; the guerillas hardly ever use anything but their feet.

"There was a good example of this the other day, in what we call Resistance Zone D. After sixteen B-52 attacks the US command declared the area a 'White Zone'—that is to say, wholly devastated. In point of fact our total casualties were eight oxen killed. The Liberation men are still there today, and somewhat reinforced.

"Mr Macnamara has recently put much confidence in mobility. He has described his new 1st Mobile Cavalry Division as the strongest and swiftest division in the history of the nation, and he is probably right. He has about a thousand helicopters. What he always forgets is that in three years the Liberation forces have learned how to handle helicopters, which can be very vulnerable at between ten and twenty metres up. You can safely say that we no longer fear helicopters.

"We are now well into the dry season, when the Americans reckoned their superiority would begin to tell. The idea was to scatter the guerillas with the Air Force and thus prevent face-to-face encounters, while the big military waves penetrated into the liberated areas. But it is now two months since the dry season began, and the Liberation people are still in the ascendant.

"The new strategy of our people is: to ensure both a concentration of force and guerilla tactics; to attack in the mountains, and also in the enemy's rear, and to attack in many places simultaneously. They are now occasionally contriving to do all three at once. It seems that the dry season favours us too.

"It is the case that the present resistance fighters are incomparably better than we were in the French time, and we were clearly not bad then. We have, however, grown more mature.

"Our own help, from the North, grows; this I do not conceal from you. The Americans claim that three divisions of our regular Army have been identified in the South; I can assure you that this is nonsense. To send so many troops from the North is just unnecessary; there is more than enough manpower already there; we provide training, cadres, equipment. Not so much equipment as you might think; the Americans and the puppets are good providers. I cannot of course inform you of the strength of our aid.

"We are well aware that the forces against us are stronger, and richer, and infinitely more powerful. We have already had great losses, and I am afraid we shall have greater yet. The price of all this is horrible. But quite honestly I do not see how we can lose. How long it will take I do not know. I may not see the end myself. But I expect my children will.

"I wonder where they are. My family is from the South. I have not seen them for ten years."

* * *

There was much in what this officer said that accords little with evidence offered by doubtless experienced witnesses of the campaign in the South. I record, however, just what he said.

NEW READERS START HERE

THERE COMES A point, and this is it, when some brief examination must be made of the background to this situation into which I had come. I do not propose to offer the definitive capsule guide to the historical curiosities of Vietnam; this purports to be reportage on a current and possibly evanescent situation and has no greater pretensions. But even reportage is permitted to invoke for its interpretation of the present some account of the past. This will be necessarily and agreeably brief.

William Warbey, MP, whose relations with Hanoi are marginally more fulsome than mine, has made the interesting comment that Vietnam as a whole is a country analogous, in size and shape and historical terms, to Norway, assuming that Norway were a country turned back-to-front, with its coast on the east instead of the west. They are both elongated, wasp-waisted territories with bulges in both north and south. flanked by sea on one side and mountains on the other, geographically associated with strong neighbours who have frequently threatened their independence. The northern borders of both Vietnam and Norway march with those of a major power that is now Communist but which, in an imperialist past, sought to dominate them. Their southern extremities reach into waters contended over by other nations. Both the Norwegians and the Vietnamese have long and enduring and individual cultures, which have been preserved in the face of many political vicissitudes. They are of almost identical size—125,000 square miles, which is almost half again as big as Britain.

From here the analogy breaks down in human terms; there are four million Norwegians and some thirty million Vietnamese. And in no circumstances would it be possible to mistake these citizens for each other.

It is useful to bear in mind that the significant part of Vietnam is not an incoherent jumped-up tribal society, but a community whose history, confused and turbulent though it is, predates the Christian era by at least three centuries. The Chinese ruled it, off and on, for a thousand years; the French for eighty, and the Japanese during their period of occupation during the Second World War. The inevitable development of nationalism and hostility to foreign rule—in this case French—began to find political expression in the 1930s. It had already thrown up a young Vietnamese scholar called Nguyen Tat Thanh, later to be known as Nguyen Ai Quoc, which is to say Nguyen the Patriot, who, having concluded that the successful revolutionary must be a man of international experience, set forth to travel the world. It turned out to be an exile that was to endure for thirty-five years, until he was to enter his country again at the end of the Second World War to organise the uprising of the Vietnamese against the Japanese invaders and their French assistants. He was by now a veteran Communist, and bore his third, and finally celebrated, name: Ho Chi Minh.

It is an odd recollection that after the war Ho Chi Minh appeared to have great faith in the United States' sponsorship of Vietnamese independence. During the war his rebel organisation, the Viet Minh, had worked closely with the American Office of Strategic

Services, the OSS; the US had supplied their arms and supported their ambitions. The wartime Power Alliance, by now the United Nations, had made many promises relating to post-war independence; it seemed that Ho took them seriously. When, in September 1945, Ho announced his Declaration of Independence, he lifted most of the rhetoric from the US Declaration: "*All men are created equal . . . certain inalienable rights . . . life, liberty, the pursuit of happiness.*" It was the first independent Vietnam government in eighty years, and the first one in a thousand years that was not a monarchy. Instead, to be sure, it was Communist.

It lasted no time at all. The task of accepting the Japanese surrender and of maintaining order in the south of Vietnam had been assigned to the British. They rapidly came into conflict with a Vietnamese population who seemed determined and eager to extend to the South the independence and nationalism already decreed in the North. The British, confronted by an anti-colonialist situation to which they reacted perhaps intuitively, ordained that the French troops be re-armed, and set to work establishing the counter-revolution, restoring the colonial status quo. The seeds were sown for the harvest we reap today.

The United States, initially apathetic about the whole business (which must have seemed to them at the time ineffably trivial and meaningless), was at that moment suddenly seized by the trauma of the Cold War. William C. Bullitt, who had represented the United States to the French Government-in-Exile during the war, had met the dispossessed Emperor Bao Dai, and become obsessed with the belief that Ho Chi Minh and his Liberation Government of the North were the outriders of a vast Communist Chinese aggression over all Asia, if not of the whole world. His words carried much weight, and do to this day.

It is tempting to develop this theme, and outline the gradual progression by which the Western world—almost imperceptibly, and in every instance for the worst of reasons—became involved in the total imbroglio of Vietnam, a country for which no statesman, American or European, in reality gave a damn, other than as a symbol of an obsessive preoccupation. It bears no resemblance to anything that had been observed before; it was clumsy and cruel and thoughtless and without consideration; step by step the West blundered and floundered into a dilemma they never completely comprehended and never in fact sought; from the very beginning they argued in clichés, wholly ignoring the fact that they were dealing with a nation that was, in fact, populated by people who knew far more about this sort of chicanery than any kind of John Foster Dulles, and who were in no circumstances going to accept a "nationalist" government established by fiat of a foreign power just to accommodate the requirements of somebody or other's basic policy of anti-Communism.

It may well be the case that another sort of Vietnamese revolution sufficiently vigorous to counter that of the Communists might have been, in the long run, advantageous to everybody; this we shall probably never know. But such a thing was inconceivable unless it had conformed and responded to the needs of the people of Vietnam, and nobody thought much about them. To this day practically nobody thinks about them. For years the total preoccupation of US policy took not the least account of the interests of the Vietnamese, but only that of the abstract compulsions of the "cold war consensus," and the angry, despairing theme of the East–West confrontation.

This was one thing, oddly enough, that few Vietnamese allowed to obsess them. It seemed to me, and I saw a fair amount of it at the time, that what about 98 per cent of them wanted to do was to get in their crops and feed their families; as it was in the beginning and ever shall be; it was not an intolerably complex ambition. The other 2 per cent wanted good jobs in the government, any government. And of those a not inconsiderable few wanted to *be* the government. In the subsequent and chaotic sequence of upheavals in the Saigon administration, quite a number actually managed it.

However, the detail of this developing situation, intricate and absorbing though it may be, is not within the compass of a minivolume written against the clock. In a word, the colonial powers contrived to restore the regime of the little playboy Emperor Bao Dai (who was known, I remember, as the "King of Cannes") and this remained until it was finally destroyed, together with the French Colonial Army, by the battle at a hitherto unheard-of place called Dien Bien Phu. Finally the whole thing was finalised, or so in our weary innocence we thought, at Geneva in the summer of 1954.

We have heard a great deal more of the Geneva Agreement in the last few months than we ever did before; the world was so sick of the endless debilitating and humiliating Indo-Chinese War that it was relieved to see it ended, without too much thought for the future. What the Geneva Agreement did is very simply defined: it put a stop to the dragging and unwholesome campaign that had been draining both France and Indo-China dry of money, men, and hope; it divided

Vietnam at the 17th Parallel of latitude—temporarily, it insisted—into two almost equivalent halves, which were to be united two years later after national elections supervised by the UN. It set up an apparatus for, as it said, ensuring both the peace and the unification of the country. It provided for the disengagement of the two opposing armies and their withdrawal into two zones of regrouping. It prohibited, specifically, any kind of military reinforcement of either zone or the establishment of any new military bases, either in the North or in the South.

Certain doubts crept in with a section of Article 14 which said:

> Pending the general elections which will bring about the unification of Vietnam, the conduct of civil administration in each regrouping zone shall be in the hands of the party whose forces are to be regrouped there in virtue of the present agreement.

Section D of the same article said:

> Any civilians residing in a district controlled by one party who wish to go and live in the zone assigned to the other party shall be permitted and helped to do so.

This provision, which covered a period of three hundred days, was the base of the migration of refugees that was to be such an important factor in the development of United States policy in Vietnam.

A tremendous wordage has been written about the Geneva Agreements, especially of late, and a certain amount of uncertainty still seems to linger over them. It is, indeed, occasionally argued that the agreements were never technically signed at all by the powers;

they therefore do not exist. The fact is that the fundamental Agreement on the Cessation of Hostilities in Vietnam was signed only by the representatives of France, and of the Viet Minh, the resistance force—which was reasonable since they were the belligerents, and the people who were instructed to administer the two territories during the interim period of separation. When the French and the Viet Minh signed the accord, that was the end of *their* war.

The perspective of history proves how little it did for the Vietnamese people; how Geneva only froze the war at its least desirable phase, and left a country bruised and divided.

However, the basic accord was "noted" by the nine delegations at Geneva—France, Britain, the US, the USSR, Cambodia, Laos, the Viet Minh and the Saigon government. It was "approved" by eight of them. John Foster Dulles, who had boycotted the talks all along and sat glowering at them from the sidelines of Paris, entered a demurrer. Three days after the conference, in July 1954, he said at a news conference: "One lesson is that resistance to Communism needs popular support, which means that the people should feel they are defending their own national institutions."

This could in theory have hardly been a more reasonable statement. In the light of what has happened since, it has a queasy ring.

The paragraph of the agreement outlining the basic political intention has been so overlaid with argument and interpretation that it might be as well to record it:

> The Conference declares that, so far as Vietnam is concerned, the settlement of political problems, effected on the basis of respect for the principles of

independence, unity, and territorial integrity, shall permit the Vietnamese people to enjoy the fundamental freedoms, guaranteed by democratic institutions established as a result of free general elections by secret ballot. In order to ensure that sufficient progress in the restoration of peace has been made, and that all the necessary conditions obtain for the free expression of the national will, General Elections shall be held in July 1956, under the supervision of an international commission composed of Member States of the International Supervisory Commission, referred to in the agreement on the cessation of hostilities. Consultations will be held on this subject between the competent representative authorities of the two zones from 20 July 1955 onwards.

I have had this quoted at me verbatim a dozen times in Hanoi. It sets forth, they say, an internationally agreed condition of affairs that is the precise definition of what they require, neither more nor less.

The elections, of course, were never held. It was believed by the United States, almost certainly correctly, that if they were to be held, under the supervision of no matter whom, they would be won by a thundering majority by the Communists. President Eisenhower wrote in his memoirs later that it was virtually certain that at least 80 per cent of the people of Vietnam, in the South as in the North, supported Ho Chi Minh. Therefore a popular election would return the wrong party. Therefore a popular election must be prevented. Therefore a "strong" and unchallengeably anti-Communist administration must be established in Saigon. What would happen thereafter nobody could imagine, but at least the worst would be staved off, for the time being.

This was the origin of the American-sponsored installation as ruler of Vietnam—initially as premier, subsequently as president—of the phenomenon called Ngo Dinh Diem, whom that excellent authority Denis Warner has called "The Last Confucian." The Ngo Dinhs were the premier Catholic family of Vietnam, once part of the mandarinate of the Imperial House. Diem was a very peculiar character indeed—religious, withdrawn, bigoted, inflexible; manifestly on the right side. He wasted no time in consolidating himself by most vigorously crushing all sources of opposition—anti-Diem nationalists, militant Buddhists, all the stray cadres left behind by the Viet Minh (later to be known as Viet Cong). There was clearly not the remotest chance of the popular mandate required by the Geneva Agreements being provided by him, nor was it, nor has it been. But Diem was just the beginning.

In 1957 Diem paid an official visit to the United States. He had by then crushed the sects and the opposition politicians and had secured the US commitment to finance his regime and sustain his army. He was red-carpeted all the way. He was flown in by President Eisenhower's personal aircraft, the "Columbine," and the president met him at the airport. His visit was handled by the public-relations firm of Oram, and the American Friends of Vietnam. He addressed a joint session of Congress. He occupied a place of honour in St Patrick's Cathedral in New York, where Bishop Flannery's sermon declared: "The entire world acclaimed him when this God-fearing, anti-Communist and courageous statesman saved Vietnam." Mayor Wagner described him as "a man history may yet adjudge as one of the greatest figures of the twentieth century." Diem's star rode high.

When he was presented with the Richard E. Byrd Award for "inspired leadership in the cause of the free world," Diem made a comment that may have been less than inspirational, but was candid. "Your aid," he said, "enables us to hold this crucial spot and to hold it at less expense to you and less danger to the world than you could have done it yourself."

However, he later told the *Reporter* magazine that he was "but an instrument of the invisible hand of the Lord." The United States press adored him: Ngo Dinh Diem was the author of the "miracle of Vietnam"—the Diem government had turned back the threat of Communism by initiating vast programmes of economic and political reform, and markedly improving the lives of the people. During those euphoric days of the late 'fifties and early 'sixties the United States press and the United States Vietnam lobby contrived to sell to themselves and to their nation the proposition that American aid-and-advice had finally produced a viable "nationalist alternative" to Viet Minh Communism, and that South Vietnam was surging forwards towards political stability and economic independence.

How fundamentally that was mistaken is visible today.

For the four years up to 1958 it is true that Diem's administration established a certain stability over parts of South Vietnam. It is equally true that the composition of those parts was seldom definable from one day to another. It was even further true that whatever Diem was managing to do he was doing through an almost completely totalitarian attitude to the business of government. The kindest thing that was ever said by his critics of Ngo Dinh Diem, and his strangely cohesive Catholic family clan, was that they "believed in democracy, but felt compelled to ration it."

From the start Diem was perfectly overt in his use of political force and social terror to strengthen and sustain his rule. There were big anti-Communist renunciation campaigns; thousands of people merely suspected of sympathising with or even approving of the other side were despatched to re-education centres; anyone held to be a Viet Cong agent was shot. Uncomfortable parallels developed between the regime of "the instrument of the invisible hand of the Lord" and that of the early days of Communist China: rewards were offered for the denunciation of parents or friends; statistics were compiled on the number of those who confessed. As it turned out, it confirmed a law of diminishing returns.

Now it so happened that there was a provision in the Geneva Agreements—Article 14c—that protected the rights of anyone who had exposed himself on one side or the other during the war. "Each party," it said, "undertakes to refrain from any reprisals or discrimination against persons or organisations on account of their activities during the hostilities, and to guarantee their democratic liberties."

How much store Diem put upon this provision is hard to establish, since he did not permit the International Control Commission to investigate any of the charges that were made of violation against this provision. After trying for some time, the commission threw in its hand, noting: "The Commission is therefore no longer able to supervise the implementation of this Article by the Government of the Republic of South Vietnam."

Again, it has to be restated that the object of the

agreements, arrived at equally by Communists and non-Communists alike, was to embody at least one or two precepts accepted, if not cherished, by the "free world." Diem had never signed them, therefore Diem renounced them. There was an occasion when the 6th Interim Report of the Control Commission said that the Viet Minh had offered "complete freedom of movement between the two zones." Whatever may have been the devious motivation of this (since every proposition from the other side was held by Saigon to have a "devious motivation") it could never be put to the test, because the South rejected it. And indeed in the summer of 1955 there were public demonstrations in Saigon against the Geneva Agreements, and the hotel that lodged the Control Commission was burned.

It was obviously in the interests of the Communists to respect the agreements as much as possible, since they were relying on the Control Commission to institute and supervise the elections, which were what Geneva had been basically all about. It has appeared that to some extent they did; the commission reported that: "the co-operation by the two parties has not been the same. While the commission has experienced difficulties in North Vietnam, the major part of its difficulties has arisen in South Vietnam."

The early objective of the United States in South Vietnam was politically complex, where now it has become militarily simplicist. It was, of course, to contain Communism, and to that end the military aid poured in. Nevertheless it was claimed by American policy makers that they had learned the lesson the French had failed to learn, and that they would not make the same mistake. From the start they claimed that their aim was a modern and democratic state of

South Vietnam, and to some extent the nation became a laboratory for a number of American political-economic theories on the advancement of backward countries. The American relationship with the undeveloped peoples would primarily be one of technical assistance —with which no one could quarrel, except that the very word obscures the political complications inherent in the involvement of such widely different cultures.

The early American personnel in Saigon tended to be men of comparatively liberal and humane views professing interest in the development of an efficient and democratic society, with efficiency taking precedence, in the hope that democracy would follow. The order of priorities was: first, security; second, technological progress, and third, the immediate benefit of the people. Thus the US Operations Mission reported with pride the kilometrage of new roads built and airfields opened, when as lately as 1958 more than half the villages had not so much as a first-aid station. Five thousand villages had no schools; they would come, it was said, by 1970. Meanwhile, they were training a thousand policemen a year.

The Vietnamese Bureau of Investigation, the VBI, was organised as Diem's secret police. While the Americans dug wells in the villages, they also built an "Interrogation Centre." Eight of the first thirty cultural officers were police advisers. It was five years before the Malaria Eradication Programme was begun; in the meantime there was an opportunity to fingerprint the entire population.

In a word, Diem was able to maintain a comparatively stable state of affairs in the South under this umbrella, and also because the Viet Minh were applying only a minimal pressure, certain that the elections ordained by Geneva would bring them victory anyhow.

Only when the Communists had abandoned any hope of those elections did they move in, militarily and politically and seriously. That meant the end for Diem, though he may not have foreseen the nature of its coming about.

It would be possible to continue for a long time about the ramifications of this dynasty of Diem; it is unnecessary because, while his oppressive phantom still haunts Saigon, the man himself is no more. He was overthrown in 1963, and died the same day of a condition so elaborate and oblique it could hardly have been publicly defined anywhere other than Vietnam: they called it "accidental suicide." In fact, he was shot in a truck by one of the rebel officers' junta. Still, "accidental suicide" may not be such a bad definition after all.

Thereafter governments of South Vietnam began succeeding each other with such erratic rapidity that nobody but specialists could keep track, from week to week, of who was running the place at all, and it became seriously difficult for fairly experienced people, like foreign editors, to name the current headman.

The United States, who continued for a while to shuffle and re-shuffle, with flagging optimism, a shop-soiled pack of minor politicians and officers on the make, soon abandoned control of the situation, asking only of their marionettes that they should show a manifest determination to oppose the North, and maintain some sort of level of recruitment for their army.

We are, however, not concerned here with the muddy entanglements of the South of Vietnam. It is enough to say that for reasons that would never be equally accepted by South and North, for motives that are of necessity interpreted differently by different people, the gradual, halting, and then swiftly mounting and multiplying involvement in Vietnam has now reached a point where it threatens all people. It has gone on for so long that whatever meaning it ever had has been lost in the deepening ruin of one side and the vitiation of political purpose in the other. Nothing is heard now but jargon. Nothing is done, on either side, but in the name of this or that concept of "freedom"—of all causes to fight for the most fatuous, since nobody knows what it means. Listen to the GI in the jungle defining "freedom" in the fatigued and wooden cadences of Dean Rusk. Listen to the Communist cadre in Hanoi defining "freedom" in the leaden clichés of the party phrase-book. Let us have done with "freedom" as a clarion-call; while the war endures the only men who know it are dead. As I write this, just back from the place, I know that this is a cruel and wretched war by now almost petrified in its own recriminations, so much so as virtually to have acquired an existence of its own, generating its own death-wish.

AT THE BAY OF ALONG

ON MY ARRIVAL in the North—indeed, long before my departure—I had of course been asked to list what aspects of the country I particularly wished to see; I had obviously listed virtually every aspect I could possibly think of, from a detailed examination of the SAM sites to a trip down the Ho Chi Minh Trail. I had also been sane enough to include great numbers of those affairs which I supposed would be acceptable, and indeed would figure on the list of all visitors' itineraries—the factories, the crèches, the civil-defence centres, and so on. After a number of years of intruding on new and self-conscious socialist societies I had developed a certain understanding of what aspects of their development are considered "useful," as they put it, and what are not. In the East particularly it is extremely important not to put people in authority into the position of having to say "no"; to be driven into a direct refusal is a painful embarrassment to an Asian; a direct refusal of anything, even of an abstraction, is offensive to all the conventions of social behaviour. A negative therefore tends to be enveloped in a tremendous amount of circumlocution, which is excessively time-consuming, and in these new days of haste and hurry is resented by all hands as a bore. Hence the number of visitors to difficult capitals who insist first of all upon being taken round the art galleries.

On this occasion, however, I felt the situation was

unusual and unprecedented enough to justify a few short cuts. Therefore among the very early requests I made was that of a visit to the eastern coastal region, the port of Haiphong, and the region of the Bay of Along. I had been told by all those who claimed to know anything about the North Vietnamese that the chances of their agreeing to let me into that area were small indeed, since in the matter of security it was held to be one of their most sensitive and important; the place was studded with installations, they said, and various considerations involving high-level security; it was furthermore a delicate meeting-ground between the Chinese and the Russians, and for Hanoi to let me in there—and with cameras, if you please—was improbable, to say the least.

However, I asked to go there, because I was especially anxious to revisit the Bay of Along.

Years and years before I had paid the briefest visit to that part of Indo-China; it had been accidental. I had put down for some unforeseen reason in Haiphong, and I had looked at the Bay of Along for perhaps half an hour. It seemed to me then, as it seemed to me now, a piece of physical scenery that is perhaps the most sensational, the most dramatic and breath-taking in all Asia, if not indeed in the world. My memory of it was of something so bizarre that I knew it could not in reality exist as I recalled it. I very much wanted to see it again, and this was almost certainly the only chance I would ever have in my life.

After three weeks they let me go there.

The road from Hanoi to Haiphong used of course to be one of the best and most conventional highways of the region, a simple drive of about 150 kilometres through the flat moist plains of the delta. Now it was the usual considerable performance: the waiting until nightfall, when darkness permitted the country traffic to move, the stocking up of the jeep with food against the conceivable emergency that would hold us up a night, or several nights, the formalities at the check-points at the city boundaries—always, with the British passport, the furrowed brow, the telephone-call; after long delays, the final friendly smile.

And then the long and wearisome progress across that great alluvial network of the delta, where the land seemed to exist on sufferance, between the multiple tributaries of the Red River; the ferries—at every one a descent from the truck, a confirmation of passes, a purchasing of tickets, a groping stumble through the darkness on to the boat; the rejoining of the convoy; so the hours went by. One worked all day, and one rode all night.

So we came at last to the Bay of Along, and there was a hotel, small and evidently new: L'Hôtel de la Baie d'Along, which had clearly been built for visitors, who may come one day.

There is nothing in the Bay of Along except the bay, but there cannot be anywhere else where one can see its like. I am surprised it has not somehow been established in the anthologies as one of the wonders of the world. It is about fifty miles of fantasy—of a thousand islands, lagoons, reefs, creeks, of little mountain-tops rearing from the blue water in a fashion so capricious that one distrusts its composition from the hand of nature alone; it is a theatrical set created by some demented and inspired designer of Oriental seascapes. Great coastal junks slid by under sails like the wings of bats. The bay does not belong to this century; it does not really belong to this world. It is even pretty;

one may use the word; yet it is gripping beyong imagination. One wished it peopled with mandarins, acrobats, concubines, empresses, poets and bearers of palanquins. It is, in fact, peopled by coal miners, sampan owners, and soldiers.

Just on the other side of it, a few miles away, lay the American Seventh Fleet.

The next day I was allowed to travel into the bay on a boat. This was a considerable concession. Strangers did not take boats into the bay, and special permission had to be sought for anyone to move on its waters before dusk. This would have been useless for me; I wanted to take film. After a great deal of demurring, and argument, and consultation, a boat was found and off we went. I had been wanting to do this for years.

At this point a brief word of professional explanation is inevitable. I was, with my two companions, trying not only to observe and explain this mysterious country, but also to film it cinematographically, and to record its sounds. It was, indeed, for this purpose that we had been admitted, or so I understood. It was also for this reason that an observation even closer than usual had to be kept upon us! *I* had no complaint at this; the presence of foreigners in any country under the conditions of war would have been regarded the same way. In the normal, or semi-normal, conditions of Hanoi and the interior no especial problems presented themselves; this was different; this was where Vietnam edged on to the ocean; the enemy was barely more than minutes' flying-time away, cruising on the other side of the islands on the flat face of the China Sea.

So spectacular was this bay, and in such a curiously obsessive way had the place impressed itself upon me, that I felt it somehow quite necessary to get in on the setting. Here it is necessary to intrude a technicality, of no significance: in the manufacture of these documentary motion-pictures it is from time to time useful to intrude what is known as a "camera-statement"—that is: the exhibition of the narrator on vision, declaiming on the sound-track some banality or other against a background recognisably local and appropriate and which is supposed to have some relevance to the burden of his lines. I believe that this has no larger motive than to prove that one did, at least, personally visit the place about which one professes to speak with such authority.

I thought it would be helpful to do such a camera-statement against the background of the Bay of Along, arguing that the startling beauty of the setting would compensate for the likely lameness of the words. I persuaded the cameraman on the advantages of such a proposition.

It was less easy to persuade the guides and watch-dogs. The idea of taking photographic gear out into the bay at all had caused much misgiving. There appeared to be a great deal on its landward side that was much involved in security—not that one could detect anything other than the normal misty beauty of the Tonkin coastline, but perhaps a technically skilled photo-analyst might have done. It was necessary that the camera-frame included as background just a given amount of harmless seascape, and when the boat was finally put to anchor out among the islands the shot was scrupulously lined up to include no more.

At this point yet another troublesome trade factor had to be taken into account. Ours was a film-unit only in the most miniature sense, since it consisted of only

Malcolm Aird who was shooting the film and Romano Cagnoni who was shooting the stills. It fell to me, therefore, to operate the sound equipment. (In the very unusual circumstances in which we found ourselves the union would, I knew, give me their dispensation; it was either that or no show.)

In the past, on locations hither and thither about the world, I have in common with most people in the film business chafed at the scrupulous fuss and insistences of sound engineers; I am unlikely to do so again. I made a very poor showing. The processes involved in filming a synchronised-sound sequence would be too elaborate to describe, even if I had a really coherent idea of what they are; to control them when oneself is attempting to make sense before the camera requires a performer with a minimum of four hands and at least two brains. Repeatedly I would go through the motions of slating the shot with the clapper-board, switching on the machinery, checking the modulation, assuming an acceptable demeanour, and then forgetting my words. Alternatively I would deliver myself of a well-turned phrase or two, only to find that I had left the microphone some ten feet away, or that I had forgotten to switch the machine on, or that the batteries had run out. Only, it seemed, was it by the blindest fluke that everything worked at once.

I recount all this tedious detail to explain why, sitting on our anchored launch in the middle of the stupendous Bay of Along, it took me about six takes to achieve anything even faintly useful as a camera statement. And by the time we had succeeded in accomplishing something, the boat had imperceptibly swung around at anchor on the tide so gently and so far that we were now pointing in almost exactly the direction we had been forbidden to approach.

Some residual sense of responsibility, or perhaps apprehension, required me to draw attention to this. Nobody minded. The guides squinted along the camera-line, and observed that the composition still included the same bollard, the same line of the boat's prow, exactly as it had been originally approved. Nobody noticed the changed character of the background.

The interesting thing is that, in the finished product, nobody ever will.

High above the bay and the port of Honggai lies North Vietnam's nearest approach to an industrial complex, centred around the big coalfields of Cam-pha. The mine itself is a stupendously big open-cast working, a huge hole in the ground about half a mile across, terraced and layered and thumping with the sound of machinery. It was operated with an odd combination of modernity and antiquity: immense Russian contraptions waddled about biting into the coal with great steel grabs, chewing out ton-sized mouthfuls with ear-cracking growls and crunches and depositing them into Russian trucks of vast dimensions. At the same time squadrons of women in the local pyramidal rice-straw hats scurried around among all these enormous wheels and grinding tracks carrying the coal in baskets at each end of the shoulder-pole, as everything all over Asia has been carried for generations. They looked like mice running about between the feet of elephants.

This big enterprise must be the only coal-mine in the world that not only overlooks but is intrinsically part of a fantastic beauty-spot. The mine is high on the coastal hilltops, and below is the Bay of Along, which from that eminence seemed even more stunning than from sea-level. There must be three thousand islands in that forty-mile sweep, each one shaped at variance to the next, with cliffs and arches and strangely formed trees, with lagoons of erratically shifting colour, and reefs occasionally uniting one part with another as though the whole formation were some titanic necklace thrown at random into the sea. It is impossible to compare the Bay of Along with any other spectacle I have ever seen; it seems literally unique. What a tourist attraction it could one day make—the place that one now has to plead to be allowed to see.

On the hillside above this hypnotic scene were the guns, embedded in anti-aircraft emplacements that must, too, have been the only ones of their kind, since they were made of coal.

Back over the ferries thirty miles to Haiphong, the east coast seaport which is, after Saigon, the biggest in Vietnam. It always was, for Vietnam, a dreary place; it had none of the meretricious corrupt luxury of Saigon or the torpid grace of Hanoi or the rural dignity of Hue and Dalat; it was a sort of Oriental Swansea. The old Cat-ti Hotel had been greatly spruced up, however, and was renamed the "Tourist." The "Tourist"! It served a very delicious mess of local crabs, which was one of the few passable dishes in Vietnam. It also claimed that the Haiphong variety of the *Lua Moi* rice vodka was superior to that of Hanoi. That was a debatable point; it could hardly have been worse.

For some days I had been promised a special treat, which was a visit to the animal factory. Mr Thing and his friends had spoken of the animal factory in tones of great respect; this was one establishment that would convince me that the North of Vietnam was a progressive nation. I considered this in terms of rather apprehensive speculation, because I could not imagine what on earth it could be—some strange and ominous breakthrough in biological experiment; some awesome variant of an Oriental broiler-farm? I could get no proper explanation from my friends—an animal factory, why, what should it be but a place that manufactured animals? Was that not correct usage?

When I finally got there the mystery was dispelled in a very commonplace way: that animal factory was in fact a misplaced emphasis on the English syllables: it was an enamel factory, and there it was busy turning out all those enamelled tin bowls and jugs and plates that were the staple commodity of all State Stores, in colours and designs that made one wonder what had happened to the celebrated Asian sense of aesthetic values.

They were very hospitable, and put on a concert at which many, and indistinguishable, patriotic songs were sung. Before I left they presented me with an enamelled tin cup of the kind I thought had been out of production since the First World War. It was decorated with the customary design of a young lady in a helmet pointing her rifle to a position overhead in which an American aircraft was falling in a wreath of pink and green flames. In this design they had very ingeniously incorporated my own name.

In Haiphong, to my surprise, I found the club still in business. The International Seamen's Club of Haiphong was once one of the memorable rendezvous of the Far East; mariners used to speak of it as of the Long Bar of Shanghai or the Waterfront in Hong Kong; it had been a great place for the traders and tramp sailors and gamblers and general adventurers of the China Sea. I had imagined that in the new circumstances it would have petered out as my little dives in Hanoi had petered out, but far from it.

In keeping with the new administration's attitude towards all institutions rooted in the wicked past, the club had been formalised, tidied up, made respectable, disinfected of all the raffish qualities that must once have made it so dubious and so delightful. It now had something of the air of a dockside tavern that had recently been taken over by the YMCA.

When I got there, moderately late by Vietnam standards, about 7 p.m., first impressions were indeed severe—a couple of Rumanian sailors were playing ping-pong, two men sat in a corner reading old copies of *Pravda*, someone else was staring fixedly at a showcase full of plastic combs. The beat of music persisted, however, and indeed the clink of glasses, and by and by I found myself in the *grand salon*, which now resembled an international seamen's club less than a recital in the Wigmore Hall. There was a thirty-piece orchestra which played what seemed to me very adequate Mozart, there was a group of Thai folk-dancers and—at last—the *ao dai* gowns, worn by what obviously couldn't have been hostesses, but which looked uncommonly as though they might once have been. Waitresses hurried around with bottles of Vietnam beer, which is conveniently called *bia*, and which seemed to be the only word of Vietnamese anyone could speak.

For the customers were still, as of yore, international seamen, though less so than long ago, since they were almost without exception from Eastern European ships in dock at the time: Russians, Poles, Rumanians, sitting observing the entertainment with a demure circumspection most unseamanlike. Among them I found

—much to my surprise, I don't know why—two British officers from Hong Kong. They both came from Cardiff, and had been living in the East for more than twenty-five years. Their tramp steamer operated on charter; if somebody wanted them to work in and out of Haiphong that was all the same to them. No, they knew nothing about the country, the Seamen's Club was as far as they had ever penetrated into North Vietnam; they claimed to have no curiosity about it.

One of the eccentricities about the club was its currency: one paid for one's drinks or bought the rather mediocre odds and ends from the "International Shop" with odd little notes called "goods coupons" which (*most* surprisingly in the People's Republic of Vietnam) were not only printed in English, but issued in denominations of, of all things, the Hong Kong dollar. "This coupon," it said, "is only valid for any expenses at Haiphong Quangninh Ship Chandler Corporation shops." This must be one of the really lesser-known ways by which the North of Vietnam raises foreign currency.

But here, too, the night-life made no excessive demands upon one's social stamina; by ten o'clock the show faded out, and the groups of international seamen returned, stone-cold sober, to their ships. In the morning the sirens would almost certainly sound; there was an air-raid alert almost every day in the Haiphong coastal region, since beyond Haiphong lay the wild reefs and shoals of the Bay of Along, and beyond the bay, the Seventh Fleet. At the time the sorties were continuous. No bombs had fallen on Haiphong, but they were falling all around. One day, everyone said, the Americans would mine the harbour, and that would put paid to the International Seamen's Club, and a good deal else besides.

But in the meantime it was back to bed, until the loud-speakers awoke one with a crash of greetings and exhortation; an enormous harsh voice jolting one into shuddering wakefulness. "Let us make this a record day of production!"

At least no one in Haiphong needed an alarm-clock.

At half-past ten the sirens went. Within minutes the big park area in the centre of town was immobile and silent, except for the whistles of the air-raid wardens chivvying the ignorant or the careless into shelters. A few eluded them, and hid under bushes, or scurried across the street holding a frond of leaves over their head. Soon the town looked as though it were engaged in a long siesta. By and by the loud-speakers began, repeating the advice to take cover, occasionally giving a running commentary on the state of the raid—how many planes Intelligence had reported, what type they seemed to be, where they were. It occurred to me that this was a far from useless service; we could have done with this sort of information during the London raids a generation before.

The alert lasted more than two hours, but nothing was audible to me except the thud and mutter of guns very far away.

That evening, however, there was some excitement; Mr Thing reported that during the day six planes had been destroyed. (On the morrow it was learned from the radio that the Americans admitted to the loss of three.) And the next day the excitement became quite real: we were to be allowed to go into the country and see the wreckage of one of them.

To drive anywhere outside the city in daylight hours

was in itself a great concession, and it was with some sense of occasion that we bumped off into the province in our overcrowded truck, out from Haiphong among the rice-fields and the vegetable patches. We drove about forty miles south to a sudden side-road that led another half-dozen miles to a village called Xa Dung, in the district of Vinh Bac. It was clearly seized with an unmistakable sense of gala. I could see no aircraft, but something had obviously happened; the village dignitaries were in conclave in a very purposeful way, and the children were running energetically around in all directions.

I asked where the wreckage might be seen, but this threw the guides into a kind of abstracted impatience. "Wait, wait," they would say, "there are difficulties." This at once aroused my misgivings, and put my mind into its protective gear of resignation—this was too often the way it began: there are difficulties, something had gone wrong that would never be admitted: this was not the village where the aircraft had fallen, there never had been an aircraft; it was all a great mistake for which no one would ever be blamed except perhaps myself, for having wanted to come; the enterprise would peter out among grumpy and resentful silences.

None of this came to pass, as it happened; I had underrated the tremendous complications of retrieving the wreckage of a high-performance military aircraft brought down in such circumstances. Such a machine does not crash; it disintegrates. It falls in pieces that are sometimes considerable, but occasionally not much bigger than a postcard, and its fragments are dispersed often over many miles, losing themselves in the flooded paddy-fields.

It was this that was causing the delay. The villagers had been out for many hours of yesterday and all today prospecting for the debris of this plane, which had been, twenty-four hours before, a B-50. A considerable part of it had already been located, and was now on its way back to the village.

While this was being explained to me there came from some distance away the sound of many voices; it was shrill and rhythmic; it had somehow the cadence of a crowd at a sporting event. I hurried along towards it, and found a cavalcade of some three score villagers wrestling in a state of high emotion with an aircraft engine.

To get this back to the village was extremely difficult, for the engine—a shapeless lump of flanges and protuberances and pipes and chambers—was extremely heavy, and the peasants were attempting to manhandle it in the only way they had ever manhandled anything, with thick bamboo lifting-poles. Every few yards along the track the poles would part with a loud crack, and more would have to be found. The path was less than two feet wide, and people were forever falling off into the flooded fields. I plodded along in the water up to my thighs; there was no room for me in this ceremony.

Very gradually and with a great amount of shouting and laughter and mixed commands and enthusiasm, the bit of wreckage was edged along, hanging between the bamboo poles. The small boys capered ahead, clapping and singing. The rest of the villagers came out to meet it—two old men were brandishing rusty old swords that must have dated from eighty years ago. As this strange exultant procession shuffled along it gave an irresistible impression, an analogy: with the villagers humping this mangled lump of metal from their poles, singing and chattering, it was the tribal ceremony of bringing back the great beast's corpse, the trophy from the chase, the communal triumph of the weak over the strong.

By the time we shuffled, drenched with sweat and slimy water, caked in mud, the other villagers were trotting in from other directions bearing other parts of the aircraft—fragments of fuselage, tangled components from an undercarriage, unidentifiable tubes and struts and spars and tangled wiring, and the painted number, bent and scarred: B-50. With great ceremony everything was carried into a large hut—it was a grain storehouse; the rice still lay about in piles—and piled up anyhow in a great clattering stack of scrap. It is the United States custom to stencil the commander's name on the hull of his aircraft, and this too had been found—I will not give his name, though I studied it with some care. He too had been found, the village commissar told me; he had not escaped; he had been buried that morning in the corner of a field some quarter of a mile away. What was left for his memorial was the fragment of metal bearing his rank and name, and very soon that disappeared under the mounting tangled pile of the debris from his final ride.

RENDEZVOUS AT THE PALACE

"I HAVE THE impression that we have met somewhere," said Mr Pham Van Dong, "which is clearly impossible."

It was nothing of the kind; it was nevertheless hard to believe that the prime minister of North Vietnam could have recalled that briefest of encounters eleven years before, in the Hôtel Beau Rivage in Geneva, in the curiously improbable company of Chou En-Lai and what was then Mr Anthony Eden. At that momentous time of the Indo-Chinese conference he had been by far the most interesting and speculative figure, representing the revolutionary Viet Minh organisation that after seven and a half years had finally got the French Colonial Empire on the ropes—and who, under the venerable President Ho, was running the state now.

I had been in the North for some weeks before I could establish contact with Mr Pham Van Dong. I had, naturally, made a request to see both him and President Ho Chi Minh from the moment I arrived. The reply from the president's staff was a categorical refusal. The President Ho regretted that he would not find it convenient to see me during my stay in Hanoi. This, at least, was something definite; in Asia one grows accustomed to equivocations and evasions and postponements—the great man will receive you some day, when convenient, when propitious; and then he never does, until the time comes to go. Uncle Ho was much more definite; he didn't want to know about me.

And yet was it Uncle Ho who was being definite? Was it not likely that Uncle Ho had never heard of my request, never heard of my arrival, never heard of me, and that this was part of what was alleged to be the contemporary Hanoi game of keeping Uncle Ho on ice? Once again I remembered the rumours of his incapacity, that he had begun to flag, that quick mind faltering. It was true that he had made no public appearance nor announcement for nearly three months; it seemed odd at a time of such mounting emergency. He could, indeed, even have been dead.

Anyhow, he was not going to see me. The prime minister's office was more uncertain; he hoped to receive me some time, but I would be good enough to understand if he found it impossible. There was, after all, a war on.

This seemed reasonable. I was, after all, something of an anomaly in the country. Hanoi is not given to accepting Westerners in these days, and infinitely more meaningful missionaries than I had been given a brush-off even more steely. I was representing nobody but myself, and it seemed improbable that the prime minister would recognise a vagrant citizen of a nation that does not, for that matter, recognise him.

However, the unexpected invitation came—as everything seems to happen in Hanoi, abruptly and without warning and at the last moment.

At an hour's notice I found myself in the vast reception-hall of the Presidential Palace, that had been when I was last in Hanoi the residence of the French Governor-General of the Tonkin Colony. I had never entered it before, but it looked exactly as I had imagined it: a cross between the Ritz Hotel and the Gare du Nord.

The prime minister came smiling across the room with his curious remark: "I think we met somewhere."

Pham Van Dong is fifty-eight, the familiar character of the well-bred revolutionary, a Marxist mandarin who started in the Royal Household, and worked his way up. His father was *chef de cabinet* to the former Emperor Duys Tam.

At Hanoi University he became a nationalist, organised a strike and fled to China with the French *Sûreté* at his heels. There he met Ho Chi Minh, Asia's number one intellectual Marxist of the day. That was some forty years ago. They have worked together ever since.

From then on he dodged in and out of Indo-China and China, finally returning for the birth of the Viet Minh movement in 1941 and four years' guerilla warfare against the Japanese.

It has to be remembered, among all the mad recriminations of today, that at the end of the war his was a legal and accepted movement, with which the French were negotiating a national government. Guerillas in those days were patriots—we saw the same thing in Burma, in Malaya. Pham Van Dong, in fact, came to Paris in 1945 as a member of the national delegation, even then, to negotiate his country's independence.

The whole thing fell through, and Pham Van Dong chose revolution. He has been at Ho Chi Minh's side since that day. Now he runs the country, and the destiny of the whole macabre Vietnam war is to a great degree in his hands. It would seem that he is perceptibly taking more and more weight from President Ho—who, after all, is seventy-six.

At close quarters he had much vivacious attraction, with mournful eyes over a fleeting but almost irresistible smile. He insisted on reading to me a prepared statement in Vietnamese about the villainies of the US aggression, which turned out to be the wearisome collage of clichés that I could by now myself recite at will. Later, and talking in French, he became suddenly real.

"When we say we are going to win this war you don't really believe it. You may think that we should, you may even want us to, but you don't honestly think we can.

"And it does sound an almost impossible claim, I agree. Sometimes when I get the reports from the South about what the Liberation soldiers are doing there I have the greatest difficulty myself in believing them, they sound so exaggerated. I can only assure you that they are true. I am hardly likely to want to deceive myself.

"Of course we can't vanquish the United States. That would be fantasy, and we are not talking in terms of fantasy. We're not *trying* to vanquish the United States. There seems to be some preposterous belief in America that we are threatening them—a poverty-stricken little country like Vietnam threatening the most powerful nation on earth! We are trying to get *rid* of them. They're on our soil, and we don't want them there. Let them go away and the war is over."

It seemed a simple enough definition, but it was a fact that this was the first time it had been clearly made by the prime minister of North Vietnam personally, to any Westerner. I have been in a number of odd and even significant situations in my life; it was nevertheless a curious feeling to have penetrated this rococo French colonial salon, that was now the powerhouse of the Vietnam revolution, from whose doors so many others had been turned away.

"You would set out your war aims as simply as that?"

"We are fighting for a perfectly comprehensible and definable thing, which is our independence exactly as set down in the Geneva Agreement of 1954. You know as well as I do that this demanded the withdrawal of all foreign armies from both North and South. Today there are 170,000 American soldiers in the south of Vietnam. How many Russian soldiers have you seen here? Not one. You've been over the country; how many Chinese soldiers have you seen? Not one. Maybe a few technicians. We are a very poor country and gladly accept technical help. But I tell you we certainly don't want their man-power; we are *full* of our own.

"I will also say this: that if for any reason our Soviet and Chinese comrades thought fit to conclude their physical help, we still win. This is a Vietnamese fight; I am Vietnamese; I know what I am talking about.

"I agree that some of these successful guerilla operations in the South seem incredible, given the huge disparity of strength between them and the US. The fact seems to be—and I do not say this to diminish our people's bravery or skill—that the American soldiers are unexpectedly easy to fight. That was surprising. They have infinitely more arms and resources than those we in Viet Minh had to face when we were fighting the French. But I tell you, from experience, that half as many French in the South would be giving our people more trouble than the 170,000 Americans. I can understand it. If I were an American young man

I wouldn't want to fight here either. The whole situation is nonsensical and wretched."

Pham Van Dong has a remarkably mobile and tense face; he gives the impression of being under constant stress, and expressions chase themselves across it with great rapidity. Now he looked very keenly at me and said:

"I wish you could understand how simple our demands are. Since the American bombings of our country began the people have become bitter and angry, but my government's policy remains straightforward. We don't want thousands of American corpses or American prisoners. We want them to go away. We want the acceptance of the legal agreement—which, remember, *your* government not only signed, but initiated. It was a *British* Prime Minister who presided over our independence.

"But it is costing us terribly dear. I'm not acting when I say that I am obliged to cry—literally cry—at the suffering and the losses. And they will get worse, make no mistake. They will get worse here in the North. They are trying very hard with their bombing to isolate Hanoi; you know that."

"Will they bomb Hanoi itself?"

"It is very possible. I think they will."

He reverted to one of my prepared questions, which asked in effect if there were any nation or group of nations whom he might consider honest enough to initiate some sort of conference to bring a pause to all this suffering.

"If you mean your own, I am afraid no. Let me go no further than to say that the British government's attitude is now so clearly a permanent reflection of

Washington's that it can have no standing as a mediator whatever. We could well have wished otherwise, but there it is. The issue is totally simple: any nation of goodwill that wishes to contribute to a settlement here must first condemn the United States aggression, and respect the inalienable rights of the Vietnamese people. We've said it scores of times. That is what it is. There isn't any half-way about it; I'm sorry, but there we are."

At this moment a most unexpected thing happened; I looked up and saw the president, Ho Chi Minh, coming through the door and padding noiselessly across the room in his sandals—the odd, clumsy, immensely practical sandals everyone wears in North Vietnam, made out of old automobile tyres. He wore a rather smart version of the official high-collar uniform, in fawn. He was laughing quite hard at my surprise.

He had, after all, categorically refused to see me, or to send a message; I had (as I said earlier) formed the impression that not improbably the tales they told were correct, and that he was unwell, or failing, or in some way unpresentable. Now he shuffled in genially, shook hands, lit a cigarette, and grinned at my being taken aback.

Yet he made it clear that we would not be photographed or filmed, and he firmly took my microphone away.

"I just don't feel photogenic, that's all," he said.

"But you are the most photogenic man in Asia, and well you know it."

"Not tonight, my friend. Nor shall I talk politics; it wearies me. You have had hours of political talk from our prime minister; that should be enough even for you."

He spoke in English, which was clearly rusty, but far from bad.

"Do you mind? As you can imagine, I get little opportunity of practice."

But of course Ho Chi Minh also speaks French, and Vietnamese, and Mandarin, and likes to write quatrains in them all. I am always unreasonably attracted by this impulse of Asian rebels, whether they be Ho or Mao Tse Tung, to express themselves in their leisure hours (which, to be sure, were mostly in prison) in verse. It may be good verse or bad verse; for an Oriental illiterate it is hard to say, but at least it reveals something of a spirit capable of comprehending something outside the caucus. Nobody so far as I know has ever unearthed a sonnet from Harold Wilson or L. B. Johnson, and whether that is a good or a bad thing has yet to be determined.

"All poets should have a spell in prison," he said, "it greatly composes the mind."

Ho Chi Minh then poured himself out a bottle of beer, lit one cigarette from the stub of the previous one, and asked how the London Haymarket looked these days. (Long years ago, one remembered, he had endured part of his education by doing a stint at the now-vanished Carlton Hotel in the Haymarket as a pastrycook under, of all people, Escoffier.) With his wispy Asian beard and glinting eyes he had the air of an impish Chinese ivory miniature. But he refused to talk of serious things. "Come, you've had all that from Pham Van Dong."

It was, I must say, something to see him. One man had held the limelight over the years without ever appearing in it. Not every actor can dominate the show from the wings, but this one could. The name rarely hit the headlines—which was odd, since it was so conveniently brief: Ho. Ho Chi Minh, President of North Vietnam, the veteran Communist of them all, the elusive father-figure whose rarely seen presence informed every move in this most brutally tragic situation of our times.

If there was a dean of the faculty of Marxist leaders it would be this frail seventy-six-year-old scholar-poet-guerilla-revolutionary, this humorous old rebel who became a Communist almost by accident. Even his name is not his own; he had had scores of names—in his early days he was Nguyen Ai Quoc, forever on the run from the Colonial French whose rule over Vietnam he opposed, constantly in prison in the China to which he fled, an almost permanent exile who yet cost the lives of 90,000 French in Indo-China and who now challenges the huge power of the US. He held his role to be that of liberating his quaint little country from foreign rule. The only people to whom that appeared to make sense, in those days, were the Communists. Communism was a pretty bleak and arid philosophy for a delicate and gentle people like the Vietnamese, but Ho reckoned it was the only way. So, accepting this, Ho became the wiliest Marxist of them all. He now had a unique position among all the revolutionary movements of Asia, illustrated by the special title he had chosen for himself—not Chairman Ho, as I said, nor President Ho, nor even Father Ho, but Uncle Ho. Thus he signs all calls and demands to the people: it is required by Uncle Ho.

The trouble about Ho Chi Minh is that he does not fit into the accepted picture of Communist leadership, he is too debonair. He has charm which he can turn on and off like a faucet. He has something which in my experience tends to be unusual behind the iron curtain, which is the gift of fun, of detachment, fantasy, of rising above the grey desert of dogma—in short, of being what he claims to be, the Universal Uncle.

The effect of this, among the people of Vietnam both North and South, is infinitely more important than his enemies understand. United States politicians, who believe that what they are fighting in Vietnam is an army of card-carrying party-member Communists, are continually being baffled to find that at least half of their foes are confused and exasperated peasants who merely want to go back to their farms, who have never heard of Karl Marx in their lives, but who are inclined to believe that Communism must be an okay thing simply because Uncle Ho says so. This is an achievement far greater, in its limited way, than Stalin's.

I asked the president: "Do you really think you can ever win? Do you honestly think you can lick the most powerful nation in the world?"

He replied: "I've got used to being an old revolutionary. The one thing old revolutionaries have to be is optimistic. You wait and see."

Most people think Ho Chi Minh's days are numbered, as effective leader of Vietnam, that he has already arranged his succession, that he is preparing to bow his way out of the Asian rebel scene he has mastered for so long. I wonder.

It was an academic question at the time. After a while he drifted out of the room—it is curious that while his entrance was so dramatic, and his presence was so important, I cannot exactly remember the fashion of his exit; by that time I was buried again in conversation with Pham Van Dong. At a certain moment we leaped to our feet, we were led into the garden, we did a brisk promenade of the presidential policies among the rose-beds, we ran about and slapped each other on the back and smiled and exchanged excessive civilities. The court photographer was summoned up from somewhere, to record officially this cordial scene. We finished the evening in what can only be described as a blaze of amity. At the back of my mind was the reflection: well, it has been tough up to now, but this is the breakthrough; from now on I can surely ask what I like.

"It was good of you to come all this way," said the prime minister. "Try to keep a good impression. It is not easy. We do mean what we say. Try to make this known, if you can."

I said, and I still say, that I shall make it known, if I can.

I romped home to the Métropole, the Hotel of Unity, full of euphoria, to find a message from the Foreign Office that I would have to leave the country without fail at six the next morning.

It is not the easiest system in the world to understand.

NORTH-WEST PASSAGE

I AM NOT at all sure why after all the cordiality at the Presidential Palace I was given my *congé* so abruptly. There was no suggestion of reproach about it; Mr Thing and his colleagues remained on the best of terms. Indeed, one of the parting ceremonies was the handing over of our thousands of metres of film, undeveloped. I had been obliged to accept as a condition of entry that I would submit all footage shot for processing and examination, and, implicitly, control. Nothing happened. To the last hour of my stay I was in despair that, not having seen any of our film, the authorities would detain it for inspection, and I should never see it again. But on the final day they came and said, in effect, that we had behaved correctly and done as we were told and not photographed bridges and fortifications and so on, and that in these circumstances we could, as a mark of signal trust, take out all our reels untouched. I am persuaded that the truth behind this was that they had only found their technical resources incapable of handling the laboratory work, and that this was a graceful way of saving face all round. However that may be, it was a vast relief.

The suddenness of my dismissal, I think, had no special undertones: it was merely a difference of procedure. Communications—never the strongest point in Hanoi—had possibly failed between the Foreign Office and the prime minister. It may be that the authorities had merely wearied of us. It may be that they wanted our guides and counsellors for other duties. It may be that they had not anticipated our receiving such a warm welcome at the palace. Or it may be, as I like wistfully to think, that this warm welcome was a form of consolation-prize for our dismissal. In any case, at half-past five the following morning we were up and packed and ready. We bade enthusiastic farewells to everyone available at the hotel—to the room-boys, the porters, to Madame Beautiful in the bar, to the little fire-eating manager, to the Bulgarian attaché, to the clerks to whom I, with great ceremony, paid the bills. It is a liberating feeling to leave an establishment where you know that you can in no circumstances tip anyone. We shook hands and embraced everyone in sight and said, with little conviction: *Au revoir*.

By six we were at the airport. By seven we were still at the airport, and likewise by eight. There was much fretful coming and going and soft discussions in corners. By eleven we were back in the truck and heading again for the hotel.

After many long and frustrating years among the airlines this was not a wholly new experience for me; nevertheless it produced its own especially fatuous anti-climax. The fond farewells of a few hours ago appeared somewhat foolish, and the expressions of everlasting amity were not easily renewed after less than a morning.

After lunch we repeated the valedictory performance again, with more hilarious insincerity, and drove back to the airport.

Four hours later we were still there. Everyone was considerate; to begin with they assured us, with diminishing confidence, that it would not be long. Only when doubts became obsessions did they admit at last that the plane would not leave at all. It seemed that the city had been under warning for an air-raid alert since dawn, and that the pilot of the Chinese Airways plane, with what seemed to me shrewd reason, preferred not to take off into the potential course of a possible squadron of the US Air Force.

No such squadron was to appear, but by now it was too late to leave.

So our dispirited ensemble was obliged once again to return to the hotel.

By now the situation had degenerated into farce. Our friends on the staff of the hotel surveyed our second return with a glum resignation. To recapture all that mutual affection for the third time running was too much to ask. They gave us back our bedrooms with a sad smile.

Now after many weeks in North Vietnam the delay of a day would not seem to have been of much consequence, but it happened that it was of dismaying importance to me. They had booked us back as our tickets indicated—that is, by way of Canton and Dacca and Karachi and Rome. A delay of twenty-four hours meant that all those reservations, all down the line, ten thousand miles of them, were lost. There could be no more for a week at least.

By now I had come to feel that another week in the Thong Nhat Hotel would be well-nigh intolerable. I could, moreover, justify that by recalling that we had, in any case, been told to go. I therefore took what seemed to me even at the time to be rather a gamey decision: I went down to the airways office and asked to be re-routed through Peking and Moscow. We had, after all, our Chinese transit visas; I considered that there would be no insuperable difficulty in securing a transit visa from the Soviet consulate in Peking.

It seemed, in Hanoi, to be surprisingly simpler than I had imagined. There was a service to Peking, by chance, the next day; furthermore, we could get on it. At Peking, said the man, there should be no special problems.

Thus it was, at dawn next day, we slunk from the hotel, avoiding the eyes of those to whom we had of late sworn such ostentatious friendship, and caught the plane. That night we were in Peking. Little did I know, as they say in the books, what I had let myself in for.

* * *

A recurrent nightmare for years has been to find myself abruptly and unexpectedly in the dead centre of some really vast and impenetrable and politically difficult place, like China, caught in some lunatic way without a visa—abandoned and inexplicable in the heartland of somewhere in which bureaucracy was supreme, facing an infinity of hostile bureaucracy, without, as they say, one's papers. It is the Kafka situation which—having sometimes glimpsed its threshold—has especially haunted me.

The corollary bad dream has been to be walking through the middle of some wintry land, amid immense uncountable fur-clad crowds, oneself dressed in casual summer elegance, as for tennis.

On this occasion both things actually happened.

The consular official in the Soviet Embassy in Peking was a good deal grumpier than most, but he agreed to let me have the transit visa to Moscow through Siberia, on production of the ticket. This, of course, I still had to obtain, since all I had was a great wad of tickets valid for a journey in quite the opposite direction. I also had a mountain of film equipment for which the excess baggage charges, amounting to some £1,300, had been paid—but also for the opposite route.

The Peking office of the Chinese Airlines was peopled with a staff of outstanding courtesy, and most generous with encouragement and advice, but only in Chinese. To come to terms with a ticket-transfer transaction of this complexity was far beyond the power of any of us present, even had there been a minimal method of communicating amongst ourselves. After an hour of trying, with much vigorous work on the abacus, a rather high official was sent for who spoke enough English to say that they would issue the ticket, on production of the visa.

From the airline office to the Soviet consulate is a long way, even by the fatiguing standards of Peking, and I cannot remember how many times I traversed it before this chicken-and-egg situation was resolved, by the unexpected capitulation of the consul. This small triumph was soon forgotten in the terrible discovery that awaited me back in the airline office.

It now seemed that, while the Soviet visa was correct, my Chinese visa was ruinously out of order. It had passed the scrutiny of the officials in Nan-ning and Peking airport, but it was left to the airline official to appreciate that while it was a valid transit-and-exit permit through the ports of Canton or Shanghai, it said nothing at all about Peking. In fact, it barred

Peking. And the Canton date had now expired. I had, in fact, no right whatever to be in China at all. Giving me my ticket was out of the question. The situation was unprecedented. What was I going to do about it?

I said he might well ask; what could I do about it? He replied, greatly exercised, that this was clearly a matter for high government consideration. I should repair with all speed to the Aliens' Department of the Foreign Office and see what, if anything, could be done about it. He did not wish to be optimistic. But there was occasion for haste, he pointed out, as time was getting on and the government departments did not stay open for ever.

I had galloped half-way down the street before I remembered that I did not know where the Aliens' Department was, nor even what it was called. Back at the desk I fretted in a fever while they rediscovered the official, who seemed alarmed that I was not on my way. I bade him write the address in Chinese characters, and rushed off again. It was now or never, since the plane left at daybreak.

I was trembling with cold. The temperature in Peking had long since sunk below freezing; already it lay in the dusk under a coat of rime, and I was dressed as for Hanoi, Dacca, Karachi and the rest in the only garment I had: a tropical linen suit. Passers-by, deep in their cotton-padded overcoats and fur hats, examined me with curiosity, as they would have done some exotic and demented creature. I was far too worried to care.

Somehow I found the building, and even the office, a place of transcendental bleakness, where three blue-clad women sat like sphinxes on a rostrum high above me. It was exactly like a setting for an unusually cheerless production of *The Trial*. Between them the officials had no word of English. They had not the remotest notion of what I wanted, and observed my anguished gestures and jumpings-about with Oriental bureaucratic distaste. One of them, on some impulse, handed me down a form printed entirely in Chinese. I began desperately to write my name on it, the traveller's Pavlovian reflex to all forms, and was stopped at once; it appeared that this was a form that had to be *filled up* in Chinese. I suspected that it was perhaps an application for Chinese citizenship, or a licence to drive a pedicab.

It was now clear that I could remain in that office for ten years without making an inch of progress in any direction. Furthermore the thought suddenly occurred to me that the production of my passport would reveal to these gorgons that I was probably the only human being among the teeming seven hundred million who had no right to be in China at all, and where that might lead I did not wish to contemplate.

By now I felt that I was beginning to lose all grip on reality. It was now a quarter past five, and all offices closed at five-thirty, and when anywhere closes in Peking, it closes. I foresaw a fair certainty of not catching the plane, and that was bad enough. A worse prospect was a frenzied lifetime of trying to make the People's Republic of China, the world's most populous state, believe that all I wanted my discredited visa *for* was not to stay, but to go.

There flashed to my mind a memory of one place from which I had from time to time received intelligible advice: the Tourist Office.

Everything in Peking is miles from everything else, but the Tourist Office is forever. The Great Boulevard must indeed be about the longest straight street in the world, and this night, in the growing dark, it stretched to infinity. I made the Tourist Office as it was about to wrap up for the night, and I was received curtly by the lady supervisor, who was clearly in no mood to over-fulfil her norm on my account.

What group was I with? No group. What was my delegation, then? Well—no delegation, as a matter of fact. Come, she said, of which department are you a guest? Unhappily I said that so far from being anyone's guest, I was rapidly running clean out of People's Money.

This obtuseness exasperated her. Foreigners *had* to be somebody's delegate, or group, or guest. However—show me your passport, she said. Her exasperation now took on a hint of anger. She indicated the visa—here, in black and white and red, it was written for all to see: no exit from Peking. And—of all things—no entrance either. This was worse than irregularity; it verged on the insane. Why in heaven's name had I not checked the visa?

I explained through chattering teeth that however decorative a piece of calligraphy it was, to me it was a pretty picture and totally incomprehensible, as I could not read Chinese. Then why had I not had someone read it to me? I muttered humbly that it had been read and re-read by officials at Nan-ning, at Wu-han, even at Peking itself, and nobody had objected until now.

That, she said brusquely, was an impossibility.

Then how, I asked, was it that I now found myself in Peking, in this predicament?

Ha, she replied, that is what *they* will want to know. But meantime I am sorry, it is closing time.

There was nothing left now but surrender. Outside in the archaic little Skoda taxi the woman driver sat asleep, buried in her great padded coat, padded trousers, padded hat. Aroused, she looked again with incredulous pity at my quivering form in the tropical suit. Thin flakes of snow were already falling. The great bulk of the Tien An Men Gate loomed against the darkness. I was freezing, and fatigued beyond care. Once again we traversed Peking to the airline office.

When the official was finally found he said blankly: "What did you do?"

I said: "Nothing." I dropped the passport on the desk and sat down like a sack of cold blanc-mange.

"But you cannot leave by the aeroplane without the correct stamp on your passport."

"So it seems."

"Then hadn't something better be done about it?"

"If you can think of anything."

"What you need," said the man, "is this," and he took up a stamp and impressed it very deftly on the passport. "*That* is the permit."

I stared at him with numb red eyes. "And you made me go— You sent me out . . ."

"When you were here," said the official, "all you did was jump about and cry: 'What shall I do? What shall I do?' " He looked at me kindly. "You never said to me: 'What will *you* do?' "

It is hard to tell with some Chinese if they are smiling on your side or not.

"The bus will come for you at five-fifteen in the morning," he said. "Have an enjoyable journey."

Well, it was a journey. It was probably the only

journey ever undertaken by three thin men through Irkutsk, through Novasibirsk, through Omsk, through Moscow, through the heart of Siberia in midwinter with the glass at twenty-nine degrees below, all smartly linen-clad, as it were for tennis.

Already Hanoi seemed a long way off.

TAKING STOCK

I GOT BACK to London in a fair condition of physical and mental fatigue; I had been doing this sort of thing for long enough to be surprised at how taxing it seemed to have been. It was nevertheless necessary to embark immediately on a period of tremendously intensive work. It seemed important to get some journalism published as soon as possible, partly because I thought the story had some right to be told quickly, and partly because the little ensemble of which I had been a part needed the money in a hurry to get us rid of the debts we had incurred. Both the *Evening News* of London and the *New York Times* were good enough to say that they could take a series right away, indeed immediately. This greatly pleased me; they are both not only among the most civilised newspapers of their respective countries, but they are organs of a most established respectability and held in regard by a public that might not ordinarily have felt it proper to be interested in reportage from Hanoi. I felt complimented that they held that there was a *prima facie* case for trusting my impressions and conclusions. They would also help pay the bills.

Nevertheless the production of the copy was a sweat of some dimensions. It could not have been called a labour of love, but it was a labour of anxiety, of impatience, and of some indignation.

Shortly thereafter I was invited by the Columbia

Broadcasting System to go over to New York and take part in the CBS annual end-of-year show, which on this occasion was to be called "Where do We Stand in Vietnam?" Naturally I jumped at it: I love short trips to New York; to me it is the finest three-day town on earth.

There is no especial point in recounting the details of the occasion, except to say that it says a great deal for the commercial expression of public democracy—a different matter from administration policy—that it took place at all, in the circumstances in which it did. The programme seems to have been widely watched, and while I am sure there were a few complaints from the US Establishment, most of the messages I received later from American liberals objected to its conventional character of acceptance. With this I feel bound to disagree; the company had been in no way obliged to have me on the show at all, and for the occasional moments when I was articulate there was not the slightest attempt, nor apparently wish, to inhibit me in any way at all.

It was, in a word, a gathering of the CBS's major authorities on the situation, presided over by Charles Collingwood, that dean of television mentors, the Curzon of the contemporary air. I say it with respect and affection. The rest of the cast was equally star-studded: Eric Sieveright, Marvin Kalb, Harry Reasoner and—flown in from Saigon, which was the other side of *my* moon—Peter Kalischer and Morley Safer. I took it that if my role was to be thrown to the lions I could not ask for more agreeable lions.

It turned out otherwise; I was nibbled but not devoured. I learned much from Pete Kalischer's analysis of the situation in South Vietnam, and chiefly that his assignment had clearly been rougher and more emotionally exacting than mine. Eric Sieveright, who as a Washington diagnostician these many years tends not to err on the side of immoderate or exuberant optimism, seemed sorrowfully to confirm most of what I had felt about that distracted location. It is true that at one point Charles Collingwood became somewhat stern with me, suggesting that, of the many adjectives that could be applied to me, "objective" was not one. This, as a general rule, is probably the case. I would accept Charles's broad conclusion there; in certain matters I lean towards being as subjective as hell. On this occasion I might have been prepared to dispute it. However, the definition of one's own subjectivity is liable itself to be somewhat subjective.

Later on it was considered a little improper that I should, for example, have printed the remarks of the liaison-colonel with the Liberation Front as he made them, and without qualification. Now here it seems to me a certain confusion about the "objectivity-factor" comes into the argument; it has been argued that by publishing this man's observations (which were overtly and expressly anti-American, and it would have been seriously surprising had they been otherwise) without qualifying or possibly denouncing them in the course of the interview, I was being non-objective. This comment has always in itself seemed singularly non-objective. I did not see what else I could do, since I was clearly in no position to check anything the officer said; for all I knew (or even know now) he may have been correct in his assertions. I could imagine of no way in which the military cause of either side could be affected by an expression of an attitude, or an analysis, when it had not been explicitly done before. It could be of no possible use to the North Vietnamese, and might just conceivably have been of interest to the Americans.

Similarly I was corrected when I reported my impression that Pham Van Dong was a potentially serious luminary in the coming Asian sky. Many authorities and experts on the South-east Asian scene have argued that this is a fallacy; they have been people with much greater access to the documentation of Vietnam, who have presented persuasive reasons for their belief that Pham Van Dong's authority is diminishing, just as they argue that the usefulness of General Giap, the victor of Dien Bien Phu, has equally faded away. It was said—properly—that I ignored the role of Le Duan, the party leader of the North, who was in the French days the Viet Minh organiser in the South, whose own increasing dominance in political matters is tied to his personal commitment to the success of the rebellion in South Vietnam. It is said that they were all sold a pup at Geneva, and will one day have to pay for it.

This may be right. It is likely that any nuances of change, of shifts and checks in the Hanoi hierarchy, could well be more readily discernible to students of the Asian Communist press and radio than they would have been to me, if only for the paradoxical reason that I was on the spot. Whatever differences of attitude or emphasis existed within the Hanoi administration, it is likely that the last person to whom they would be revealed, or leaked, was myself. At no time did I consider myself in Vietnam the sort of catalyst who would break down the intimate mysteries of the Hanoi administration; on the contrary it seemed to me from the beginning that I, of all people, was most likely to be handled with circumspection and discretion and to receive in official conversation the most distilled official line.

I tried to make this clear in my subsequent writing—that having got into Hanoi, it never seemed likely that I was going to blunder on some sensational discovery, nor be made the confidant of some dissident counter-revolutionary views, nor indeed be entrusted with anything that the Hanoi authorities would not have wished me subsequently to pass on to everyone; to have expected otherwise would have been the ultimate in professional naïveté.

Such naïveté is to be found, however, in the most experienced organisations. Shortly after my articles had appeared in the *Evening Standard* and the *New York Times*—neither of which is under serious suspicion as having a dangerously radical approach to affairs—*Time* magazine headed their account of my journey: "Conduit in North Vietnam."

> "Anxious to cover both sides of the war in Vietnam, the *New York Times* has tried for years to get a reporter into Hanoi. But Ho Chi Minh has consistently said no. Last week the *Times* finally ran a five-part series on life in North Vietnam, but not by one of its own reporters. It was the work of James Cameron, 54, a British freelancer, who was writing for the London *Evening Standard*. 'Failing our being able to get a man inside,' says *Times* Foreign News Editor Sydney Gruson, 'this was the next best thing.'
>
> "A tireless, didactic liberal of the ban-the-bomb breed, Cameron worked on Fleet Street papers

before he broke loose on his own. He prides himself on getting into areas forbidden to other newsmen, and he wangled permission to visit North Vietnam for a month this fall. His report is a rare eyewitness account by a Western journalist, but it leaves little doubt of Cameron's own emotional commitment: he firmly believes the US has no business whatsoever in North Vietnam. . . .

"When he is not filing background color, Cameron is less a reporter than a conduit for North Vietnamese propaganda. He all but equates Hanoi, which has not been touched by bombs, with wartime London, which was hit heavily. He quotes officials, such as North Vietnam's Premier Pham Van Dong, at interminable length, without any appraisal of what they are saying. . . .

"His articles, described as personal journalism, are full of personal prejudices—all anti-US, pro-Hanoi. . . .

"Convinced that Communism is the wave of the future in Vietnam, he does not miss a chance to tell his readers that there is no alternative to letting Hanoi have its way. Bombing, he insists, can have no appreciable effect. The North Vietnamese, he says, 'have a totally unshakable determination to win the war . . . they reject the machinery of compromise.'

"The London *Evening Standard* ran Cameron's report under a disclaimer saying that his opinions were 'not necessarily' those of the newspaper. The *New York Times* explained that Cameron was a British journalist, but offered no disclaimer for his observations. Nor did most of the newspapers that picked the story up from the *New York Times* News Service. While the *Los Angeles Times* ran only a two-column skeptical analysis of the series by its London correspondent, other papers generally played it the way the *New York Times* did: the first one or two articles appeared on Page One; the rest of the series was tucked inside. Most editors apparently accepted the reports as a fresh, factual view of the enemy. If they felt like Scott Newhall, executive editor of the *San Francisco Chronicle,* that in part, Cameron was a 'receptacle for some masterly public-relations work by the officials in Hanoi,' they did not say so in print."

So that was my comeuppance from *Time.*

If the thing had been worth arguing about the only argument I might have made was about the use of this interestingly pejorative word "conduit." I had been behaving in Vietnam as a "conduit," which I take in the especial *Time* sense to mean a sort of drain. Well, that is as may be. My definition of "conduit," in common with that of a dictionary, is a "channel." I noted down and recorded what divers people in North Vietnam said to me, including the prime minister and a hostile colonel; thereafter I printed it in newspapers, exactly as noted. It is true that I did not intersperse that record with descriptions of Pham Van Dong as a slant-eyed, evasive, yellow-skinned, and doubtless anti-American example of Asian Communism; I merely put down what he said. I have no objection to that being defined as the behaviour of a "conduit," or channel. I have been a foreign correspondent for quite a number of years, and I am obliged to say even now that if the function of a reporter is not that of a channel, then I am at a loss to know what his function is, unless it be that of writing for *Time*.

One small addendum might serve to round off the tale: the day this salutation appeared in *Time* I was telephoned in New York by the Book Publication Section of that same organisation who, it seemed, were anxious to commission me to write them a book on North Vietnam. For some reason I took this to be especially wrong that the *Time* organisation should wish to inflict on their readership a book about Vietnam written by someone whom they had only that day described as a "conduit." When I pointed this out, the man said: "Well, it's a different department."

This seemed finally to establish the fact that Mr Luce letteth not his right hand know what his even righter hand doeth. I have lost much sleep over the past weeks, but not over that. When Mr Luce begins to like you—that's the time to start worrying.

* * *

The circumstances of preparing a book like this make denouement and serious conclusion difficult; even during the preparation of these chapters the situation shifts, changes, eludes definition. The development of what was known as the Johnson "peace offensive" has become clouded with cross-motivation; there were in any case too many doubts and double-thoughts involved; but as I write the bombing of North Vietnam has not been renewed, though daily the renewal seems imminent.

It will be impossible to maintain the situation as it is.

Militarily it is preposterous. During the past year the United States forces have been increased in numbers almost tenfold; the supply routes from the North have been endlessly bombed; the Viet Cong have been attacked with every kind of formidable ordnance; and the result of all this has been that their opponents are stronger than ever before, that hardly a square mile of territory has been permanently "pacified." The Americans hold a fringe of bases round the coast, and Saigon. The "experiment in democracy" has been abandoned, and Air Vice-Marshal Ky rules by open dictatorship.

The United States therefore considers it has no choice but to meet each successive failure by driving the scale of the war up another notch to a point where they must be more successful. Long ago General Giap defined this dilemma: "The enemy has to drag out the war in order to win it, and he does not possess, on the other hand, the psychological and political means to fight a long drawn-out war."

The result of this is certain disaster.

The absolutism of the North Vietnamese sometimes puzzles those, by no means all their enemies, who believe that negotiations in some form or another are ultimately inescapable. Is their categorical refusal to talk *only* obstinacy?

It is, of course, based on many factors. To begin with Hanoi is obliged to believe that it was twice deceived in negotiations with the West when it was on the verge of gaining its political ends. After the last war, when they fought the Japanese occupation with US help, they found that the British and the Americans forced back a French occupation and swindled them out of their legitimate aspirations for freedom.

When, years later, they won their victory over the French, the Americans impeded the elections required by the Geneva Agreements. The history of negotiations has not been a happy one for Hanoi.

The men who run the Hanoi government are the same men who directed the successful war against the French; every one of the leaders has been engaged in the struggle for independence for more than twenty years. They are unlikely to be deterred or discouraged now because someone in a B-52 blows up a bridge or a workshop. As the London *Times* has said: "North Vietnam is not a proud, new, industrialised country. It is half of a country—and the tougher half by far—that wants unity and independence far more than it cares for factories. The American bombing was based on assumptions that do not necessarily apply."

Moreover, after their long history of painful occupations, it is likely that they do believe what Ho Chi Minh told the Pope: that it is the US aim to transform South Vietnam into "a military base and a new-type colony of US imperialism." Other big powers had tried precisely this; why not the Americans?

Meanwhile China and the Soviet Union contend over Vietnam, obsessively regarding the war there as another area of their own conflict. For Peking it is the most valuable opportunity to demonstrate that China alone is the true inspiration of the world's revolutionary movements; continually she urges Vietnam to fight on, regardless of cost, though her own contributions in aid have been less than that of the Soviet Union. Meanwhile Peking assails Moscow for minimising her help in the interests of an alleged secret collaboration with Washington.

The position of being an arena for this inter-ideological polemic presents its own dilemma for North Vietnam. China is inescapably part of the Vietnam background; they are parts of the same East Asian civilisation; Vietnam's nationalist movement was inspired in and organised from China. Nevertheless the present resistance could never be sustained without Russian help. It would be impossible for Hanoi to become directly embroiled politically in the Sino-Soviet struggle, and in Hanoi every effort is made to play it in as low a key as may be. This may not be possible indefinitely.

The issues grow clouded; little is seen now other than through that most unreliable of instruments, the mind's eye. It is almost forgotten that there is only one reason why the Vietnam war is unique, in both its patriotic and political aspects. It began long ago as a simple colonial struggle against the French, as there had been so many subject peoples' struggles against other occupying powers without calling up the crusading wrath of the "free world." Where it differed from all previous—and for that matter subsequent—colonial struggles was that in the case of Vietnam the nationalist leadership was Communist, overt and proclaimed. This had happened nowhere else. It is an essential difference. For the last twenty years the essence of the Vietnam fight has been more or less the same: it has been that of a colonial people for national independence, with the additional factor—either useful or disastrous, as it may be regarded—that it was organised by Communists. It is this fact that has engendered in the American mind that in the Viet Cong they are confronting, not a crowd of Vietnamese whose principal ambition is to remain Vietnamese, but serried hordes of well-schooled, doctrinaire, card-carrying party members whose closely planned objective is the eventual destruction of the United States, her constitution and her economy. If you ask many a reasonable American precisely how it is that the richest and most powerful nation in the world feels itself threatened by a small and backward South-east Asian country on the other side of the globe, the chances are you will be answered in analogies about dominoes and about the world conspiracy.

It would be fatuous to deny that there is a certain reasoning to this—though nine times in ten that reasoning is adduced in clichés that are themselves totally unreasoned—and that to some degree the imbecility is compounded by a mutual hate. Nevertheless I think we have long ago abandoned the process of defining our terms.

"But surely," I hear a television voice, not improbably that of Mr Michael Stewart, "the essence is the familiar struggle between freedom and tyranny."

All around one can see, or imagine, the heads nodding gratefully, relieved to have life clarified in a moment of revelation. Freedom versus tyranny is a rallying cry of some nobility, if one only knew what the hell it meant. Whatever it means, for both sides the bonds tighten; already fear calls up the symptoms of the disorder we fight—the intolerance of dissent, the readiness to impute guilt by association, the impatience with protest. "The tyrant fear," I once read, "pricking us to fight tyranny."

The American nation is a strong and invincible one and, I truly believe, a generous and peace-loving one, whose human reactions are intuitively kind. I have plenty of personal experience of that. It is yet possible that it has become irrational on Communism—that multitudes of Americans, including and indeed especially those in high places, have come to regard Communism not so much as a rival or contending political proposition, to be countered in political ways, but as a kind of plague, a virus, a malevolent intangible beyond the reach of argument, an intrinsic evil not to be confronted with reason at all but to be reacted to as one would react to an epidemic, by some sort of cautery of fire. Is it now possible that those who control the policies of the United States now think of "international Communism" as a veterinary doctor thinks of rabies: as something not susceptible to treatment, but as a disease that as a social duty must be put down by elimination? If that is the case then there is logic in the belief that it is possible to cure Communists of Communism by blowing it out of their heads with high explosive, and woo people into the ways of democracy and freedom by burning them up with phosphorus and napalm.

It is possible, however, that that, too, is based on assumptions that do not necessarily apply. It would all be so simple if they did.

* * *

I must acknowledge for the last time that these are the gratuitous notes of someone who feels only that the Vietnam story has been one-sided too long; I am one against a great many. I was not asked to write this; I was not even asked to go. But I did, and I hope there will be many more, with more to say, and longer time in which to say it.